The Customer and Supplier Innovation Team Guidebook

Also Available from ASQ Quality Press

New Product Development: Strategies for Supplier Integration
Robert Monczka, Robert Handfield, Thomas Scannell, Gary
Ragatz, David Frayer

The Team Based Product Development Guidebook
Norman Reilly

Supplier Management Handbook
James L. Bossert

Supplier Certification: A Continuous Improvement Strategy
James L. Bossert , John O. Brown, and Richard A. Maass

*Team Fitness: A How-To Manual for Building a Winning Work
Team*
Meg Hartzler and Jane E. Henry, Ph.D.

*Critical SHIFT: The Future of Quality in Organizational
Performance*
Lori L. Silverman with Annabeth L. Propst

Quality Problem Solving
Gerald F. Smith

Root Cause Analysis: Simplified Tools and Techniques
Bjørn Andersen and Tom Fagerhaug

*Value Leadership: Winning Competitive Advantage in the
Information Age*
Michael C. Harris

To request a complimentary catalog of ASQ Quality Press
publications, call 800-248-1946, or visit our online bookstore at
http://qualitypress.asq.org .

The Customer and Supplier Innovation Team Guidebook

Patrick H. Norausky

ASQ Quality Press
Milwaukee, Wisconsin

The Customer and Supplier Innovation Team Guidebook
Patrick H. Norausky

Library of Congress Cataloging-in-Publication Data

Norausky, Patrick H., 1938-
    The customer and supplier innovation team : guidebook / Patrick H. Norausky.
        p.   cm.
    Includes bibliographical references and index.
    ISBN 0-87389-479-0
        1. Physical distribution of goods—Management. 2. Marketing channels—Management.
    3. Business logistics. I. Title.

HF5415.7.N67 2000
658.5—dc21   99-462076

10 9 8 7 6 5 4 3 2 1

ISBN 0-87389-474-X

Acquisitions Editor: Ken Zielske
Project Editor: Annemieke Koudstaal
Production Administrator: Shawn Dohogne
Special Marketing Representative: David Luth

ASQ Mission: The American Society for Quality advances individual and organizational
performance excellence worldwide by providing opportunities for learning, quality
improvement, and knowledge exchange.

Attention: Bookstores, Wholesalers, Schools and Corporations: ASQ Quality Press
books, videotapes, audiotapes, and software are available at quantity discounts with
bulk purchases for business, educational, or instructional use. For information, please
contact ASQ Quality Press at 800-248-1946, or write to ASQ Quality Press, P.O. Box 3005,
Milwaukee, WI 53201-3005.

To place orders or to request a free copy of the ASQ Quality Press Publications Catalog,
including ASQ membership information, call 800-248-1946. Visit our web site at
www.asq.org. or http://qualitypress.asq.org.

Printed in the United States of America

 Printed on acid-free paper

American Society for Quality

ASQ

Quality Press
611 East Wisconsin Avenue
Milwaukee, Wisconsin 53202
Call toll free 800-248-1946
www.asq.org
http://qualitypress.asq.org
http://standardsgroup.asq.org

DEDICATION

To Christine, partner and loving wife.

TABLE OF CONTENTS

LIST OF ILLUSTRATIONS

Table Number   Description

PREFACE

My total absorption with creativity and innovation began nearly four decades ago. During this period, I managed and participated in significant aerospace and advanced industrial programs. I was keenly aware that cutting edge ideas were valuable only when put into practice. I championed breakthroughs that succeeded because customer-supplier innovation teams were used. Work needed to get done. People were placed on teams and expected to do their very best to reach the goals set for the teams. Results were satisfactory. But looking back, results could have been significantly better if more effective processes had been used to better identify, create, and operate the teams. In the 1960s as is now, customer-supplier innovation teams were not formally recognized. The space program represents the exception. The space program comprises only the best of the very best for ideas, people, and teams. (NASA 1999)

As the space program brings a very visual view of the globe, one wonders if anybody out there is listening to the grinding and crushing tempo created by global competition? Certainly, it's loud enough. In many cases, it is causing companies to downsize operations in order to gain greater efficiency in serving global markets. As a result, acquisitions and mergers are increasing. In fact, 23,000 deals occurred worldwide in 1998 and were worth $2.5 trillion. (Deutsch 1999) This was up from $1.6 trillion in 1997 and $1.1 trillion in 1996. (Securities Data 1999).

On one level, a means to combat global competition is the intense emphasis on the *eureka factor*. Creativity and innovation are at the forefront. Customer-supplier innovation teams offer an excellent arrangement for supply chain competitiveness.

This practical *how to* book is an outgrowth of a series of lectures and workshops over the past six years. As a first of a kind book on this topic, it recognizes the importance of bringing the customer-supplier innovation team into a more open forum as a key means for a competitive advantage.

The reader is provided with a practical approach to identifying, creating, and operating customer-supplier innovation teams. Chapters are arranged to enable the reader to learn the basic points and retain techniques by working through self-instructional exercises. A basic rule for the reader is to use this practical guide as a self-development tool and then apply the tool to the job to produce results. The Appendices contain numerous forms and examples to assist a reader in the application process. The Appendices really enhance the *how to* contribution of this book.

This book comprises nine chapters. There are abundant figures and tables to support the text. A section is included at the end of each chapter for lessons learned, a summary, and key questions. The key questions for each chapter are intended to stimulate the reader to think about the questions and generate answers needed for reform.

In Chapter 1, the importance of the customer-supplier innovation team is established as a competitive advantage. The impact of global competition is examined. Customer-supplier relationship thinking is introduced. A customer-supplier innovation team model is presented. Each subsequent chapter addresses one element of this model in detail.

Chapter 2 covers the composition needed for a sound customer-supplier relationship. Trust is recognized as the key factor for a sound relationship. A trust journey process and model are described. A scoring process for a customer-supplier sound relationship is covered with illustrated examples. The reader is provided a blank assessment form in the Appendix to support evaluation of his or her interests with customer-supplier relationships. Without the existence of a sound relationship, the success of a customer-supplier innovation team is questionable and therefore, not recommended.

Finding the right talent for the customer-supplier innovation team is covered in Chapter 3. A team selection process is presented. This involves identifying, interviewing, evaluating, selecting and educating candidates needed to form the team. Forms are provided in the Appendix to support the reader's application for the team selection process. The value of the Myers-Briggs Type Indicator® Inventory (MBTI)® and Kirton

Adaption-Innovation (KAI) Inventory instruments are discussed as a means to assist a team member to better understand his or her operational and innovative preferences.

Once team members are selected, Chapter 4 covers the process for determining the Innovation Focus (IF) and Innovation Focus Quotient (IFQ) for the team members and their sponsors. This Quotient shows where gaps exist that could create barriers to operational success. The IF and IFQ approach used in conjunction with the Myers-Briggs Type Indicator® Inventory (MBTI)® and Kirton Adaption-Innovation (KAI) Inventory instruments brings a full dimensional representation about the innovation levels concerning the team members and their sponsors. Innovation Focus questionnaires for self-assessment and organizational assessment are illustrated. Guidelines for IF and IFQ acceptance levels are presented. Examples are covered for key aspects of the process.

With the team ready, the creative process is then covered in Chapter 5. A distinction is made between creativity and innovation. When both are combined, a "solution system" exists. The creative process is covered in detail. Creative techniques that enable a team member to be creative and generate ideas are explored. Pros and cons for each technique are listed. A brief introduction about the Theory of the Solution of Inventive-Type Problems, given the acronym TRIZ (Russian designation), is introduced. The importance of capturing all data and information concerning an idea is emphasized. Environmental work factors that enhance creativity are examined. The role of diversity in the creative process is presented. The role of benchmarking in the creative process is discussed. Creativity in time-compressed situations is illustrated with the Apollo 13 example. After all is said and done and ideas exist, the issue of creative progress is covered with examples for measures, metrics, and measurements. A technique to evaluate creative ideas is presented. Only creative ideas that offer merit as candidates for implementation are moved to the innovative process. Internet web sites that support creativity are listed. Numerous worksheets and examples of techniques and steps in the creative process are contained in the Appendix.

Once creative ideas are selected, then the team progresses to apply these meaningful ideas through an innovative process described in Chapter 6. The point is made that incremental improvements impede competitiveness whereas breakthrough improvements at the innovative level better contribute to a strong competitive position in the global market. An innovative process model is introduced. Team members must function as evaluators as well as generators of ideas. This requires a mental shift. A value-cost matrix is used for transferring ideas from the creative process. Guidance on innovative idea rating is included. The influence of the work environment on the innovative process is covered. The 3M™ Trizact™ Abrasive Belts story illustrates a work environment that supports innovation. Innovative techniques are covered. Team members are provided guidance on the process of presenting innovative solutions to sponsors. The issue of "risk" taking in the innovative process is examined as a necessary step, in most cases, to obtain breakthrough solutions that satisfy the problem/situation. Examples of measures, metrics and measurements are defined for team progress. Internet web sites that support innovation are suggested. Numerous worksheets and examples of techniques and steps in the innovative process are contained in the Appendix.

Chapter 7 explores the process for operating the innovation team. Emphasis is placed on allowing the team to operate in a non-restrictive manner while yet ensuring full communication across the team, adhering to schedules, and, most importantly, producing results. Co-leader traits for successful operation are illustrated and discussed. An operational process model is presented with the distinction that management of the team and project is done separately to ensure team functionality in the creative and innovative processes. Co-leaders are provided with techniques to successfully operate from team and project standpoints. Caution is advised in using benchmarking to avoid the "We found the solution; let's stop at this minimum solution." Steps are covered that lead to filing for patents associated with discoveries in the creative and innovative processes. Numerous worksheets and examples of techniques and steps for the operational process are contained in the Appendix.

Chapter 8 covers the processes for a reward system and team refurbishment. The significance of positive reinforcement is emphasized as the building block for the reward system. Customer-supplier business cultures are examined with regard to reinforcement, recognition, and reward. The importance of soliciting and using viewpoints of team members in designing the reward system are covered. Guidelines are illustrated for the design and operation of the reward system. The pros and cons of the reward system are explored. Co-leaders are provided examples of behavior measurements for the reinforcement process. Conditions for team refurbishment are discussed as a means to boost team morale, to avoid burnout problems, and to better ensure team efficiency and effectiveness.

The team's effort is directed to produce the right results at the right time for the right reason. Chapter 9 looks at the results produced by customer-supplier innovation teams. The value of the customer-supplier innovation team model is clear. It offers the advantage of knowing *how to* and *why* results are produced rather than whatever happens . . . happens . . . That's just the luck of the draw! Prospects for the future of customer-supplier innovation teams address the issue of speed that impacts the "solution system."

The basic techniques presented throughout the chapters are based on logic and applied with common sense. Inquisitive people from a wide variety of businesses over a number of years established the validity of these techniques. However, a word of caution, use the techniques from a thinking perspective rather than in a blind fashion of *plug and crank*. Be vigilant to observe the cause and effect relationship while using these techniques. Greater benefits will result.

This book is unique since writers about customer-supplier relationships have not addressed the issues of what it takes to have a sound customer-supplier relationship, and the identification, selection, and operation of customer-supplier innovation teams. The customer-supplier innovation team model provides guidance for consistent identification, selection, and operation of customer-supplier innovation teams. This book brings together fragmented pieces to create a concise and cohesive model for customer-supplier innovation teams. Certainly the insight presented in this book contributes to an improved competitive advantage for all those who adopt the model.

It is my professional wish that this book will encourage others to engage in a more open forum about their insights, experiences, and work with customer-supplier innovation teams. Sharing advances the state-of-the-art. Everyone profits!

Patrick H. Norausky
16 Knollbrook Lane East
Painted Post, NY 14870
e-mail: glomaxspch@glomaxx.com
www.glomaxx.com

ACKNOWLEDGMENTS

My deepest appreciation to the great group of people who helped to make this book possible:

- Friends and associates: Deborah Pettry of Leadership Focus, Deborah Bodinger, John Kello of Davidson College, Department of Psychology, for comments on the foundational paper "Customer and Supplier Innovation Teams" that served as the impetus for this book.
- Longtime friend and associate Jim Kowalick of the Renaissance Leadership Institute, Inc. for his thoughts and advice on TRIZ, inspiration and intellectual foresight.
- Friend and artist Tom Vroman of Vroman Associates for his insight on creativity.
- Frank Cerminara at Hershey Foods for his perspective on procurement practices.
- Michael Kirton of The Occupational Research Centre for his professional courtesy and willingness to share information about the Kirton Adaption-Innovation (KAI) Inventory.
- Stan Collins and Blane Huppert at the 3M Abrasive System Division for the 3M™ Trizact™ Abrasive Belts Story.
- Rick Price at the Corning Museum of Glass for his willingness to share information about the history of glass.
- Pat LaLonde, Vice Chair Technology of the ASQ Customer and Supplier Division for the introduction to ASQ Quality Press and her encouragement for the book.
- Christine Jeno at GLOMAXX, LLC for her input, patience and attentiveness to detail during the preparation of this book.
- Ken Zielske and Annemieke Koudstaal at ASQ Quality Press for editorial and project support.

There's a Better Way!

"I can't understand why people are frightened by new ideas. I'm frightened of old ideas."

John Cage (Composer, 1912–1992)

CHANGES IN THE MARKETPLACE

The secret is out! There is a better way to beat global competition. Companies are scrambling to capture the last frontier—namely the creative and innovative ability of people. There is a virtual explosion of innovation. For the last several years, annual reports of companies (for example, 3M, General Electric, Corning Inc., Deere and Company) have declared innovation as the answer in all the splendor that graphic technology can provide. Inside, the reports contain a treatment and proclamation of payoffs achieved through innovations that increased profits and stockholder satisfaction.

Why are these explosive shock waves being released? Simply to combat the offensive threat of global competition. Cost pressure is causing customers to demand price-cutting from suppliers. Most customers and suppliers are rebounding in dismay and general confusion. The secret may be out, but the systems and processes are open for definition. There is hope as customer-supplier innovation teams offer an excellent arrangement for supply chain competitiveness.

Recently, while on an airplane to Hong Kong, the person next to me started talking about the difficulties he faced in keeping up with global competition. As president of a small die-castings company that supplies the automotive industry, his company struggles to meet price, quality, and delivery requirements. He couldn't understand how a company in Asia could produce the same product at a price equal to his material costs, with higher quality, and deliver to a U.S. location. Fortunately, a business associate arranged visits to several Asian manufacturers for him to learn their *secrets*.

While listening to him elaborate on his business problems, it struck me that the biggest problem he faces is himself and his attitude about running a business. For years, he supplied die-casting products to the same customer. He didn't have any competition. Then computer-aided design and analysis created a better understanding of the die-casting technology. Competitors could rapidly change their processes to fully meet shifting customer requirements.

I asked him about his relationship with his customer. He said that he does whatever the customer wants. There aren't any discussions. Neither he nor his people visit the customer to learn how their product is used as a subassembly by the customer. He said "It's like dropping the product into a black hole in space." He expressed fear that if he asked too many questions, the customer would think he wasn't qualified to make the product in the first place and he would lose the business.

After further conversation, I learned that at a bidder conference recently, he discovered that the customer was working very closely with an Asian supplier. In fact, an Asian supplier became a team member with the customer to better integrate the supplier's processes with those of the customer. Also, this enabled the supplier to provide valuable input to the customer when the customer develops new products.

This story about the die-casting executive's dilemma is typical for many businesses regardless of industry, size, product, or service. The company's leadership fails to grasp the essential factors needed to run a modern-day business. Senior executives seek to continuously apply what has worked in the past. Of course, *worked in the past* doesn't necessarily mean that it was the best or most effective system. They do not sense nor see that the world is in constant state of change with globalization as its major driver. They try to keep up with the global competition but the effort becomes one of trying to play catch-up rather than analyzing the cause and effect relationships and how to take action to change the rules of engagement.

GLOBAL COMPETITION

The difficulty with many businesses seeking a global competitive advantage resides in the absence of not addressing the key issues. Globalization is both social and financial. In many cases, companies only address the financial and either don't know or ignore the social component.

Globalization is not just a trend, not just a phenomenon, and not just an economic fad. It involves the integration of free markets, nation-states, and information technologies to a degree never before witnessed, in a way that is enabling individuals, corporations, and countries to reach around the world farther, faster, deeper, and cheaper than ever before.

The driving idea behind globalization is free-market capitalism. The more you allow market forces to rule and the more you open your economy to free trade and competition, the more efficient and flourishing your economy will be. Globalization means the spread of free-market capitalism to virtually every country in the world. (Friedman 1999).

Understanding the philosophies and principles associated with globalization sets the basis to use globalization as an economic reservoir rather than a economic vacuum sealed off from the majority of potential participants. "The ideal global company is both a low-cost producer and customer driven. It balances global consistency with local diversity. It has a flexible product and service architecture that allows for a high level of customization. It has a highly coordinated value chain that utilizes multiple centers of excellence distributed throughout the world in the most appropriate locations" (Daniels 1993).

Globalization can be a vague word. To its prophets, it promises a glorious future and unending riches. To its critics, it bodes doom. It is a catchall word that has become shorthand for a menu of economic and social changes. It certainly has to do with the growth of global trade and investment. It is most clearly seen in the development of a global financial market. It is blamed often correctly, for waves of downsizing. Its fingerprints can be seen on millions of pink slips issued to factory workers and middle managers alike. It is both more and less than the dawn of the Information Age. Not everything ascribed to globalization can be credited to technology, but it would not exist without the development of the computer, the microprocessor, and the communications satellite.

Globalization could be defined as the creation of a global economy. More specifically, it is a revolution that enables any entrepreneur to raise money anywhere in the world and, with such capital, to use technology, communications, management, and labor located anywhere the entrepreneur finds them, to make things anywhere he or she wants, and sell them anywhere there are customers.

Clearly, this is still a revolution in progress. We aren't finished yet. In some areas of this revolution, we aren't even close. A truly global economy would be a worldwide version of national economies like the American one. In such an economy, money, goods, services, jobs, and people would move as easily from country to country as they do now from New York to Pennsylvania (Longworth 1998).

As the global economy exists now, only money moves this freely. Money, in fact, moves like the trade winds. More than $1.8 trillion moves every day through the money markets of the world. It has grown from $20 billion in 1973 to $2.3 trillion (projection) for 2000 according to the Bank of International Settlements.

THE BEST BUSINESS APPROACH

The Industrial Revolution found its beginnings with each manufacturer being self-sufficient and self-contained. Suppliers were needed and used but not in widespread practice with close relations existing between the customer and supplier. Not until the mid 1980s did customers begin to appreciate and value relationships with suppliers. Customers realized that a sizable competitive leverage is possible with win-win supplier relationships.

An example of a win-win relationship is attributable to General Motors. The General Motors Truck Group established a GM-Behr innovation team based on parameters set by GM and Behr. The team is working on a new type of radiator fan clutch that is activated by a unique magnetorheological fluid. This new technology creates a competitive advantage for both companies (Baker 1998).

Industries such as automotive, energy, aerospace, communication, transportation, and pharmaceutical realize that a major key to competitiveness resides in establishing sound customer-supplier relationships. Automobile manufacturers are integrating suppliers into production and assembly lines. In this arrangement, both manufacturer and supplier make capital investments and share the risks.

In most business sectors, customers are reducing the number of suppliers in the first-tier to a critical few. In the automotive sector, the first-tier suppliers are gaining economic leverage over subordinate tiers. During the next decade, the number of suppliers redefining themselves as system integrators will more than double, creating a new first-tier. The balance of the old first-tier, or direct suppliers, will move into traditional second-and-third tier roles. The shifting of various support activities from Original Equipment Manufacturers (OEMs) to system integrators will allow OEMs to lower their break-even production quantities and to serve smaller niche markets. The evolution of OEM competencies is shown in Figure 1.1. There is concern that the economic balance of power that now resides with the OEMs will shift to these first-tier suppliers in the future (Sage 1998). Suppliers may then be in a position to dictate price and delivery terms to customers. Looking to the future, awareness and caution is suggested in order to avoid a possible irreversible situation between customers and first-tier suppliers. Further, so goes the automotive industry—so goes a model for other industries.

It is a best practice to take a relationship inventory such as the one shown in the Table 1.1 example. Considering each source of supply and the relationship with this source provides not only identification of the current status but requires answers to

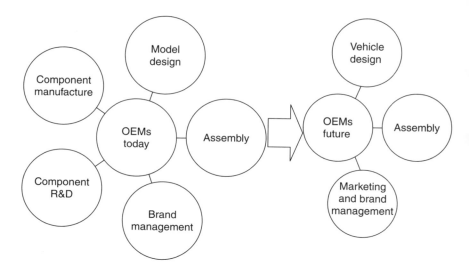

Figure 1.1. Evolution of OEM competencies (automotive).

what's needed to advance the source in the relationship and whether or not a potential customer-supplier innovation team should be further explored. A blank form for Table 1.1 is provided as Appendix A.1 for the reader's use.

This table provides a beginning for understanding any changes to the relationship. Chapter 2 deals with relationships in detail and having an inventory of the type in Table 1.1 supports facts needed for changes to the relationship.

MANY FACES OF THE CUSTOMER

Who is the customer? In many companies there still remains confusion as to the answer despite the total quality movement. The customer is: 1. any recipient of the output from a provider of a product or service or, 2. all persons who are impacted by our processes, our goods, and our services (Juran 1988).

In a supply chain system, a daisy chain exists where the roles of customer and supplier alternate as either a customer or supplier depending on whether an input is provided or an output is received, Figure 1.2.

Table 1.1. Customer-Supplier relationship inventory (example).

Organization: *Falcon Engines* **Prepared by:** *Joe Pricer, Director, Materials Management* **Date:** *April 11, 1999*

Source	Vendor	Traditional Supplier	Certified	Partnership	Alliance	Potential C-S Innovation Team	Comments
Acme Steel	X						Poor on-time delivery record. Replace source.
Computer Services		X					Encourage certification.
Tooling Unlimited		X					Encourage certification.
Hi-Tech Foundry			X				X	Seek partnership.
Standard Adhesive		X					Poor quality. Replace.
Globe Valves				X		X	Encourage alliance.
Allied Rings					X	X	Excellent relationship.
Standard Gear			X			X	Seek partnership.
Tri-State Lubricants		X					Encourage certification.

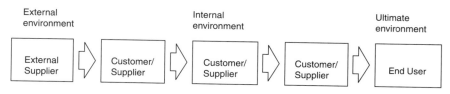

Figure 1.2.   Customer-Supplier chain.

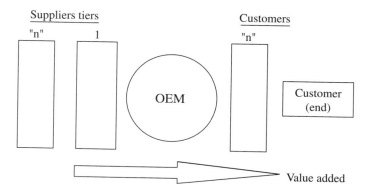

Figure 1.3.   Value-added supply chain.

A value-added supply chain is shown in Figure 1.3. From an external viewpoint, the original equipment manufacturer (OEM) or service provider can function as both a customer and supplier, Figure 1.3. Also, the end-user as a customer represents the user of the product or service, Figure 1.3.

Figures 1.2 and 1.3 illustrate the dependency of customer and supplier relationships. It should be noted that in Figure 1.3, the service provider could be substituted for the original equipment manufacturer (OEM) in the case where service rather than manufacturing exists.

As innovations continue to occur all around end-users, it is logical that customers will require further innovation in order to satisfy end-users. The bar continues to be raised. For example, not too long ago, a 33 MHz processor represented the latest technology for personal computers compared to the 500 MHz processor today which is already obsolete as you read this. Customers want faster processors because of advances with software pro-grams all demanded by end-users. The cycle is relentless as advances in existing technologies occur and new technologies become available.

SEEKING A COMPETITIVE ADVANTAGE

How can a company respond to global competition?

First, companies need to find effective ways to develop new products and services. The economist Lester Thurow observed: "Wealth is created by the capitalization of innovation—by linking new discoveries to customers' wants and needs" (Marquardt and Reynolds 1994).

Second, companies must find new ways of working faster and better. Duplicating the systems and processes of competitors is no longer sufficient because competitors continuously change the rules of operation. The new ever-evolving market place eliminates the chance for stagnation and duplication. To be successful, a company needs to lead rather than follow in the global business environment.

Third, companies must find new ways of working cooperatively, with customers and suppliers as partners, rather than adversaries. With the complexity of global business no company can succeed by itself, especially with slow incremental improvements to products and services that seriously lag behind market demands.

The core purpose and key advantage of a customer-supplier innovation team, then, is to develop new products and processes that enable a company to respond to rapidly-changing market conditions. Since the processes and systems cross boundaries of the customer and supplier, the team represents not only a tacti-cal but also a strategic approach to gain a global competitive advantage.

Let's look at an example of how this works:

To better understand a supplier's processes, a customer sent a team of their top engineers to a supplier's plant. The supplier manufactured explosive devices used to inflate air bags in automobiles. After several weeks of analyzing the supplier's processes and systems, the customer's senior engineer told the supplier's management team: "You are not charging us enough money for the product you sell to us." Was this engineer crazy? Hardly! He went on to say: "We expect your cost accounting system will alert you to this fact after several more months of production. We're concerned that you might decide to reduce the product's quality so you can maintain your margin and we'd end up with less-than-satisfactory product." (Norausky 1989). After additional discussion, the customer and supplier agreed to work closely together as a customer-supplier innovation team. Together, they found a way the supplier could meet the customer's requirements and still profit. If they had maintained the traditional adversarial relationship, the customer might have ended up with an inferior product or even a bankrupt supplier.

So it's clear—surviving in a rapidly changing environment requires quick response with new and effective answers. Effective innovation is the key. So what prevents companies from innovating effectively?

Sometimes, it's fear of change. A person's normal tendency is to try to maintain a stable environment. But surviving change means becoming its master, rather than its victim. As Ed McCracken, former CEO of Silicon Graphics stated: "The key to competitive advantage isn't reacting to chaos, it's producing that chaos." (Higgins 1995). Dealing with chaos is like being in the eye of a hurricane, producing the chaos makes it easier to operate—at least the producer is in the eye.

But companies that recognize the need for change often have trouble. The desire to implement customer-supplier innovation teams does not automatically imply that the necessary process steps are known or understood. In recent discussions with senior executives at Fortune 500 companies, executives expressed frustration with the inability to form teams where members aligned with the need to be innovative. Though competent professionals, team members lacked curiosity and passion to understand the business situation that they faced and to define alternatives different from the same alternatives used in the past. Because of this narrow viewpoint and their unwillingness to change and grow, they weren't able to position their company as a real competitor.

CUSTOMER AND SUPPLIER: WIN-WIN

A customer can operate its organization with a wide variety of supplier relationships. Historically, the vast majority of customer-supplier relationships were conducted in a standoff and even adversarial manner. Usually, the attitude of both the customer and supplier involved getting *a good deal* at the expense of the other party. A lot of time and resources were wasted in zero-sum games. The range of relationships is shown in Figure 1.4. Partnerships and alliances are not legal entities, but rather, mutually beneficial and open relationships wherein the needs of both parties are satisfied.

Common sense and advances in thinking about how individuals and organizations should interact to conduct business revealed that, in reality, competition exists between value chains

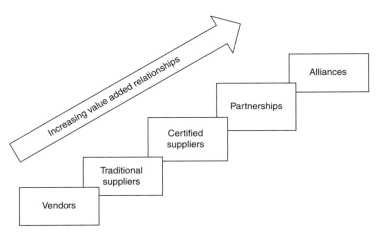

Figure 1.4. Customer-Supplier relationships.

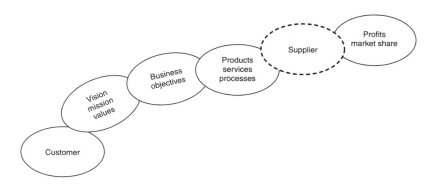

Figure 1.5. Critical importance of supplier.

and not between members of a value chain. Figure 1.5 illustrates the critical role a supplier plays in achieving profits and market share for the customer. Of course, this achievement also benefits the supplier from profit and market share standpoints. This suggests that customer and supplier should be more open with each other in a collaborative manner to achieve common objectives. Partnership and alliance relationships can then occur as a natural outcome from this principle. Relationships are built on four key characteristics: 1. common interests, 2. mutual needs, 3. willingness to be open and sharing both benefits and risks, and 4. trust. A detailed treatment of customer and supplier relationship characteristics is covered in chapter 2 of this book.

CUSTOMER AND SUPPLIER INNOVATION TEAM MODEL

The model, Figure 1.6, shows that customers' and suppliers' needs are defined by the constant change created by global competition. Ideally, a customer-supplier innovation team can change the rules of engagement in dealing with global competitors. Instead of being a follower, the team can lead and set the standard for the competition to follow. The model elements offer a path for leadership success.

One hundred thirty-four teams over the past several years validated the model, Figure 1.6. (Norausky 1998). A total of 1,206 team members from aerospace, automotive, energy, and communica-

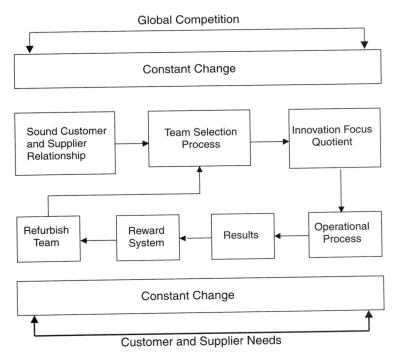

Figure 1.6. Customer-Supplier innovation team model.

tion industries participated. The seven processes comprising the interior portion of the model are covered in subsequent chapters.

This model represents a step forward from the random manner of identifying, creating, and operating customer-supplier innovation teams in the past. The processes that this model comprises are more consistent and cost effective relative to the existing random processes.

LESSONS LEARNED

1. Creativity and innovation offer the least capital-intensive approach to not only provide a competitive position but also a leading position rather than a following one.

2. Businesses cannot continue to apply what worked in the past and compete in a global marketplace.

3. Business leaders need to change their business approach rather than playing catch-up as followers.

4. The higher the value-added relationship between customer and supplier, the greater chance for a win-win success in a global market.

5. Successful companies recognize that suppliers represent a critical link in achieving profits and market share.

6. Globalization is spreading as businesses large and small are able to raise money anywhere in the world.

7. Customer-supplier innovation teams offer an excellent arrangement for global competitiveness.

8. Companies must find new ways to: a. effectively develop new products, b. work faster and better, and c. work cooperatively with suppliers.

9. Creating chaos rather than merely being part of it represents a strategy for market leadership.

10. Customers can only be successful in dealing with suppliers that support innovation of products, services, process, and systems.

11. Customer-supplier innovation teams are presently identified, created, and operated in a random manner. The model presented in chapter 1 offers a consistent and cost effective approach. One hundred thirty-four teams validated the model. Teams were from the aerospace, automotive, energy, and communication industries.

SUMMARY

1. Changes in the marketplace are driven by globalization. Globalization represents the attributes of a free-market society. The speed of transmitting data and information provides considerable balance and leverage in global markets.

2. Companies are using creativity and innovation as a cost effective means to achieve global competitiveness. After all, people represent an asset waiting to be more properly and fully utilized. The challenge is to provide people with an innovative focus and to do so as fast as possible.

3. Meeting price, quality, and delivery requirements is possible with changes to systems and processes.

4. Industries such as automotive, energy, aerospace, communication, transportation, and pharmaceutical realize that a major key to competitiveness resides in establishing sound customer-supplier relationships.

5. It is best practice to define an inventory relationship table. This table provides a beginning for understanding the state of the relationship and changes that may be needed.

6. Customer-supplier innovation teams offer the advantages to respond with innovative products, services, processes, and systems to rapidly changing market conditions.

7. Identifying, creating, and operating customer-supplier innovation teams is better achieved with the model described in this chapter. This model enables a team to lead rather than follow during a more consistent and cost effective process for the innovation of products or services.

8. Lessons learned regarding globalization, innovation, and customer-supplier innovation teams are covered.

9. The reader is presented with a series of questions regarding change, globalization, and achieving a competitive advantage.

QUESTIONS

Questions are intended to stimulate the reader's thinking about material in the chapter and necessary actions for transforming the reader's organization.

1. Why are businesses searching for a competitive advantage?
2. How has the marketplace changed?
3. What caused the marketplace to change?
4. What kinds of challenges do these changes mean?
5. How have companies responded to these challenges?
6. What is the impact of global competition?
7. How can global competition be used to better focus a company's business practices?
8. What can be done to acquire a competitive advantage?
9. How is a competitive advantage achieved?
10. Who has achieved a competitive advantage?
11. How did they achieve a competitive advantage?
12. What were the results?
13. What was done to improve initial results?
14. What case study reinforces the value of a customer and supplier working together? How is the case study presented?
15. What case study illustrates a customer providing leadership to a supplier?
16. How is the case study presented?
17. Why does a supplier need to support its customer?
18. What type of support should the supplier provide to its customer?
19. What actions can a supplier take to improve its tier suppliers?

20. What model can be used to gain a competitive advantage?

21. Why is the model for customer-supplier innovation teams unique?

22. How have the needs of customers changed?

23. Why don't companies seek the customer-supplier relationship more aggressively?

24. How does a company respond in a positive manner to a supplier relationship when only costs are important?

The Best Way to Compete  2

"The strangle knot will hold a coil well—It is first tied loosely and then worked snug."

The Ashley Book of Knots

CUSTOMER AND SUPPLIER NEEDS

A customer calls a meeting with a supplier and announces that they should establish a customer-supplier innovation team. The supplier is both surprised and puzzled by this announcement. But after all, the supplier wants to continue to do business with the customer so the supplier agrees to do what the customer wants.

Is the customer-supplier innovation team going to be successful? Most likely not! The primary reason is that the customer and supplier didn't define and discuss their needs and the influence of these needs on their relationship. The alignment of needs is essential for creating a win-win relationship, Figure 2.1.

An example of needs is shown in Table 2.1. The customer and supplier needs should be understood and alignment achieved for the relationship to progress. Differences in needs must be reconciled in terms of win-win. In typical relationships, needs of the supplier are not discussed to the point where the customer realizes that changes on the part of the customer are also required for a win-win. Customer specifications represent a good example.

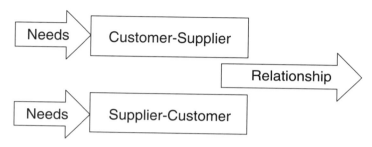

Figure 2.1. Needs alignment.

Table 2.1. Needs table example.

Need	Customer-Supplier	Supplier-Customer
Price	Competitive	Allows adequate profit
Quality	Highest Quality	Process dictated
Delivery	On-Time	On-time
Improvement	Continuous	Depends on investment
Future business	Depends on Market	Essential
Certification	Requires	Depends on investment
Incoming inspection	None	May require
Shared risk	Yes	Maybe

Minor changes may result in significant improvement for cost-effective production on the part of the supplier. Unless both parties openly discuss their needs and the impact a need creates on the other party, the best solution remains hidden.

Best of class customers and suppliers individually complete a *Needs Table* and then discuss their differences and what is needed to reconcile these differences. A blank *Needs Table Worksheet* is provided in Appendix B.1 for this purpose. It is suggested that customer and supplier begin the process with the same list of needs to be fulfilled. Additional needs can be added but at least a baseline of needs are used to start the process.

ROLES OF CUSTOMER AND SUPPLIER

Historically, the customer drove the relationship. The supplier followed. Twenty-first century business sets the roles on a more egalitarian basis. The customer creates the business requirements for the supplier but the supplier also provides input in the form of products or services to satisfy the dependency of the customer. As discussed in chapter 1, the supplier holds a critical position in the supply chain.

In the automotive industry, first-tier suppliers assume a partner role with their customer. At its truck and bus assembly plant in Resende, Brazil, Volkswagen uses trust relationships with its first-tier suppliers. Volkswagen invested some $250 million dollars to provide the basic plant infrastructure. Supplier partners invested an additional $50 million in their respective modules. Thus, this deal was configured as a basic-risk-sharing undertaking. The partners have guaranteed fixed term contracts that span from 5 to 15 years. These suppliers not only finish the production of integrated modules, but also are responsible for assembling the modules into complete vehicles. This has eliminated the need for Volkswagen to hire its own assembly-line workers. Volkswagen doesn't take ownership or pay for the components until a vehicle passes final quality inspection. "Cost reductions of at least 15 percent are being achieved and significant improvements in quality realized" (Sheridan 1997).

CUSTOMER AND SUPPLIER RELATIONSHIPS

Customers and suppliers need to establish a sound relationship before forming and operating customer-supplier innovation teams. The synergy created by this relationship enables the quantum achievements associated with innovation teams to occur. A sound relationship ensures products and services at the highest quality and lowest overall cost to the customer while providing a fair profit to the supplier. Further, it requires that the customer and supplier engage in a continuous process to remain competitive on a global basis.

Based on analysis of many customer-supplier relationships, the following characteristics define a sound relationship (Van Mieghem 1995):

1. **Trust**—Created by personal relationships, trust is the open exchange of information, and facts that demonstrate commitments are met. Trust is the keystone for a customer-supplier relationship. Also, certification by the supplier, (for example, ISO, QS) helps to demonstrate that the supplier is willing to establish a documented basis for trust. Education and training courses taken by both the supplier and the customer provides evidence that both parties are remaining current in their understanding of technologies and business methods.

2. **Effective Communication**—Communication lines exist at all levels within the customer and supplier organizations. Issues regarding price, service, and quality are addressed and negotiated up front and contracted. Active listening is used.

3. **Commitment**—The customer is committed to long-term business and volume with the supplier. The supplier is committed to cost-effective production. Both are committed to their business relationship and fulfilling their part of the contract.

4. **Strategic Planning**—Customers and suppliers conduct joint strategic planning sessions to address cost savings and innovative engineering, manufacturing, and quality contributions that extend the state of the art.

5. **Prevention**—The supplier uses preventive methods and techniques to operate systems and processes to avoid quality, performance, delivery, and cost problems. The customer uses a specification process compatible with the supplier's systems and processes for cost effective production.

6. **Co-operation**—Both the customer and supplier are willing to work to make each other successful. Both parties identify risks and agree on handling risks and sharing the consequences.

TRUST: THE KEYSTONE

A deal is closed. Handshakes occur between parties. Everyone believes that the deal between customer-supplier creates a trust relationship. It is focused to make both parties more competitive, cost effective, and profitable—a deal intended to achieve a fully integrated relationship. Wall Street analysts applaud the deal as a sound strategic move. Is such a deal necessarily unique? Does it represent a means to combat global competition? Are companies engaging in customer-supplier trust relationships? Let's examine some possible answers to these questions.

In a survey of fifty companies randomly selected from the list of Fortune 500 companies, it was determined that all fifty companies are engaged in a relationship with their suppliers (Norausky 1997). However, these relationships range from lowest cost only to a fully integrated relationship. The majority of relationships exist for the lowest cost. If only lowest cost was the reason and, in turn, this was not achieved in the relationship, then the customer was inclined to change suppliers. Of the fifty companies surveyed, only ten were a fully integrated relationship.

In the automotive industry, great emphasis is placed on the supply chain and establishing customer-supplier trust relationships. Over the past several years, Tom Stallkamp as Vice President of Purchasing for Chrysler skillfully created trust relationships with their suppliers. His effort made Chrysler the envy of the automotive industry and gave Chrysler a key competitive advantage. "Chrysler tapped Tom Stallkamp as its new president for his uncanny ability to make suppliers cut costs. He helped to squeeze billions of dollars from Chrysler's supply and development operations. However, his most critical contributions dealt not in dollars but in relationships. This involved team building among procurement and other functions, such as engineering and manufacturing, as well as among suppliers" (Minahan 1998).

In the chip-making business, Intel forged trust relationships with its key suppliers, among other reasons, to avoid a year 2000 problem. "Since the mid 1990's, Intel started working with suppliers to ensure that Intel's supply chain would be interruption-free by the Year 2000 and beyond" (Intel 1998).

A trust relationship is essential even for nontechnical businesses. "J.C. Penney depends on trust relationships with

reputable suppliers who can deliver high quality, low cost mer-
chandise to meet requirements of J.C. Penney and its customers"
(Penney 1998).

Across many industries, customer-supplier relationships are
sought and made. The ideal relationship is one based on trust.
But what is meant by *trust*? Let's examine the definition.

There are two, quite distinct components of trust: trustworthiness and trustability. Trust is a skill as well as a value; trustworthiness is the value part, trustability the skill. To cultivate
trust requires value-honesty, openness, sincerity, and skill reliability and dependability. To say *I trust you* must imply both.

Trustworthiness is manifested in sincerity and the honor-
ing of agreements. It can be developed and sustained through
personal relationships and track record, or through painstak-
ing crafting of formal contracts designed to avert misunder-
standings and provide metrics for ensuring that commitments
are met.

Trustability is essential to cross-functional process coordina-
tion in a just-in-time environment. Each party must be confident
that the other party will deliver on time and as specified; both
must avoid the plane collision problem. Precision flight teams
such as the Blue Angels must have team members that deliver
the right maneuvers at the right time. You don't become one of
these pilots unless you can fly and be trusted to deliver what is
required by your teammates.

In this regard, and as a consequence of cross-functional linkages
of processes, just-in-time operations, and customer-supplier electronic links, businesses are becoming more and more like precision
flight teams. As processes are designed or redesigned to eliminate
waste and delays then the activities and participants become more
tightly coupled and highly interdependent, breakdowns in one part
of the process immediately affect the other parts. A supplier that
can't deliver on time and meet required levels of quality won't be
trusted. An unreliable and incompetent department won't be a wel-
come addition to a cross-functional team.

"Trustworthiness demands high standards of business ethics
and frankness. Trustability demands total competence. Trust
provides the bonding and integrity for the customer-supplier to
gain power and strength in their relationship" (Keen 1997).

The quality of a customer-supplier relationship comes down to the relationship between people. The quality of these relationships is to a great extent a function of the trust that has been established in the relationship. "In behavioral terms, trust is the relative confidence one has in the predictability that an individual will do what they have agreed to do" (Patton 1997). The internal trust that exists can easily be translated externally to suppliers. The consuming public will seek products that emerge from a trust relationship. For example, Gerber baby products have over the years established a sound reputation of trust with the consuming public. There is consistency and reliability of its products. Also, for example, Campbell's soups, Kleenex tissue, McDonald's hamburgers, and Maytag washer/dryers enjoy a similar reputation of trust. What companies do you think of when you think in terms of consistency and reliability of their products?

Getting Started

Getting started on the trust journey with key suppliers should be as easy as 1, 2, 3 go! However, before charging-off, there are six areas to evaluate. The outcome of this evaluation will indicate the risk in proceeding. A program manager at the customer's company, usually the head of the purchasing function, becomes the process owner. Also, the supplier should identify a process owner.

1. **Performance history of the key suppliers and associated future performance risks.** A supplier's on-time-delivery and quality conformance records represent a basis for determining whether or not it is reasonable to proceed to enter into a trust relationship with a supplier. It is should be noted that prior history is but one view. Indicators of current performance in conjunction with a reasonable near term understanding of the supplier's operation and shifts in the management structure will contribute to a total system understanding as to the worth of the supplier. Promises by marginal key suppliers without changes to support these promises should be cause for rejecting the supplier. Bottom line, the supplier is either competent to meet customer requirements or not meet them.

2. **Input from involved customer internal functions, for example, engineering, manufacturing, sales.** All functions and associated key personnel that provide input to or depend on the input from suppliers form a critical component of the trust relationship. The focus is directed to achieve open communication from all these functions. It is intended that a realistic database exist so that negotiations can be conducted with key suppliers.

3. **Customer's and suppliers' level of willingness to engage in open exchange of information.** In a trust relationship, there are no secrets. Suppliers must provide the customer open access to all facets of their operation. And in turn, the customer must grant the same privilege to the suppliers. The open exchange must exist at all levels of both organizations.

4. **Responsiveness of suppliers to support changing needs of the customer and to resolve problems.** In most cases, suppliers will need to make capital investments of buildings and equipment to ensure the customer requirements can be met. Suppliers rely on the integrity of the customer that the supplier investments will provide a financial return besides being guaranteed a level of business with the customer.

5. **Suppliers' commitment to engage in a continuous improvement effort.** Suppliers make continuous process improvements that result in measurable improvements involving reduced cycle time, improved product quality, and scrap and rework reductions.

6. **Customer willingness to accommodate needs of suppliers.** The customer must continually evaluate its own operations and requirements that impact suppliers. In many cases, the processes and requirements used by the customer may not be compatible with the suppliers' product input. The customer must be willing to make changes in the same manner that the customer expects the supplier to make change provided the changes contribute to the common advantage of the relationship. The supplier must trust that the customer will be as critical of its own operations and requirements as the customer expects from the supplier.

Getting started by evaluating the six points covered above will ensure that both customer and supplier are engaged in a trust journey and that such a journey is advantageous to both parties. Open and honest communication provides a valuable key for getting started in a trust journey. When risks are identified then both parties can determine the actions needed to either eliminate or minimize these risks. "The principles for 'Getting Started' apply equally to large and small companies and across all industries." (Lewis 1995).

Process

This section covers the process for the trust journey. The insight gained from understanding the process will contribute to process implementation by organizations new to the process and, depending on the situation where a trust journey already exists, the possible revision of an existing trust journey process.

The trust journey process is shown in Figure 2.2. As mentioned in the previous section, "Getting Started," there are two process owners for the trust journey: one at the customer end and the other at the supplier end. The process owner at the customer end is the primary *driver* of the process since in the majority of cases, the customer is the initiator of the trust journey.

The model for the trust journey is shown in Figure 2.3. The two key points in the model are the levels of maturity to reach in the trust journey and the continuous improvement of all aspects of the relationship.

The levels of maturity are defined in Table 2.2, which provides a system perspective on the levels of maturity that exist with a supplier relationship. It is important to note that a supplier can be a primary/top supplier yet be at a beginner level simply because the supplier is new and a track record hasn't been established. This situation occurs continuously in high technology industries where new products and service are being introduced and suppliers possess little or no track record. For example, a manufacturer of optical couplers requires the latest sub-components that can only be secured from a primary supplier that is virtually a start-up company with a great technology but no track record as a supplier.

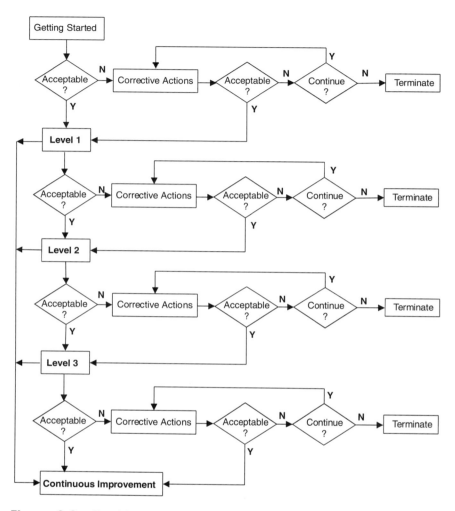

Figure 2.2. Trust journey process.

In talking to key people at customer and supplier organizations, one of the topics raised was the issue of determining . . . "How is the trust journey validated?" Validation occurs when evidence is compared to accepted criteria that indicate a trust relationship exists. For example, after a period of time, a supplier became late in meeting delivery schedules and the quality of a product began to slip below required levels. The customer was caught by sur-

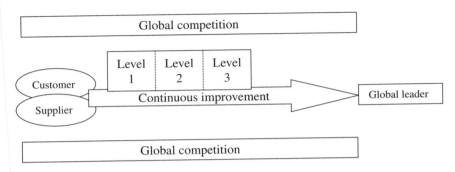

Figure 2.3. Trust journey model.

prise. When an investigation was conducted to determine why this occurred, it was learned that there was a shift of managers at the supplier. Additionally the management team the customer had initially formed the trust relationship with had completely changed. The supplier did not notify the customer of this change. The supplier shifted operational emphasis and the trust relationship, in essence, was informally dissolved on the part of the supplier. From this and similar cases, it was determined that validation needs to be an on-going process. This creates a contradiction as to the value of a trust relationship in the first place. The trust relationship in theory should be self-maintaining. In reality, there are too many variables and circumstances in a dynamic business environment that suggest being conservative and not attentive in a trust relationship will enable unchecked problems to occur and be disruptive. Points to follow in the on-going validation process are:

- Quasi-real time communication between supplier and customer. *No surprises* regarding changes in management structure, manufacturing processes, reductions in markets at either the supplier or customer end that cause reduction in personnel.
- Trend analysis of real-time data acquired from the supplier's electronic database.
- The financial soundness of the supplier and customer.

    The founders at the customer and supplier organizations who establish the trust relationship must remain involved. Though

Table 2.2. Levels of maturity.

Item	Beginner Level 1	Intermediate Level 2	Mature Level 3
Trust	Top and 1st Tier	Top plus 2 Tiers	All Levels
Open Communication	Key People	Partial At All Levels	All Levels
Cost savings	Minimum Required	Above Minimum Required	Substantial
Value Added	Below Required	Required	Exceptional
Continuous Improvement	Some Operations	Majority of Operations	All Operations— Aggressive
Response to Market Shifts	Slow	Somewhat Flexible	Very Flexible
On-Time Delivery	Major Exceptions	Minor Exceptions	Always Meets Requirements
Product/Service Quality	Major Exceptions	Minor Exceptions	Always Meets Requirements
Validation	90 Days	Annual	Not required
Self Initiative	When Suggested	Partial w/o Suggestion	Completely on Own
Innovation	Apprentice	Practitioner	Expert at Break-throughs

Table 2.3. Gap determination.

Item	Customer View	Supplier View	Gap
On-time delivery	Only 95%	Acceptable	Resolve 5%
Quality	Only 80%	Only 90%	Resolve 10%
Cost	Additional 20%	Acceptable	Resolve 20%
Innovation	Lacking	Great ideas	Resolve lack of innovation

other people in both organizations participate in the trust relationship, these founders must remain engaged in the trust relationship. This becomes very important when major issues occur and fast resolution is required.

In seeking to improve communication, a gap identification method can be used. This method involves both parties answering a series of questions based on their view of acceptable performance. The answers to these questions are compared to determine the extent that a gap exists. Once gaps are identified, a corrective action plan can be defined to resolve differences. An example of areas to formulate questions for the gap analysis is provided in Table 2.3.

Legal

In the business world of yesteryears, deals were made entirely on the basis of a handshake. Today, a trust journey needs to be predicated on foundational requirements that each party agrees to honor without being reminded. These requirements are defined in terms contained within a legal agreement that both parties sign. This agreement protects the interests of each party. Items such as proprietary information rights, change of ownership, breaking the agreement, operations in other countries, and financial responsibility are covered. "The uniformity in legal rules when engaging in global business is provided by the United Nations Convention on Contracts for the International Sale of Goods (known as CISG)." (Murray 1997).

As a general rule, it is wise to have a legal audit of the inner workings of both the customer and supplier organizations and operations. The findings can provide a benchmark as the customer-supplier proceed on their trust journey.

An excellent example that tested the validity of a customer and supplier trust relationship occurred because of the requirement of computer systems to be year 2000 (Y2K) compliant. Customers needed to avoid being jeopardized by suppliers who were unable to meet delivery and product quality commitments. For mission critical suppliers, in-depth audits and test results were required. Customers had to trust that suppliers would become Y2K compliant. "Suppliers involved in trust relationships were expected to take all actions to prevent a liability issue for their customers" (Intel 1998). Looking back as the clock turned from December 31, 1999, to January 1, 2000, both customers and suppliers were relieved that the Y2K requirement was met—a true testimony for a customer and supplier trust relationship.

Pros and Cons

There are pros and cons associated with the trust relationship and associated journey. An example of these pros and cons are shown in Table 2.4. As a general rule they apply to all trust relationships.

Table 2.4. Pros and cons.

Pros	Cons
Share technological and financial risks.	Circumstances may cause partner not to honor agreement.
Ability to react faster to market changes.	Legal agreement may be costly to terminate.
Better position to reduce costs.	Performance may decline.
Long term relationship agreement.	Relationship requires validation to ensure compliance.
	Obsolete technology may be used.

SOUND RELATIONSHIP

In a sound relationship, the customer sets expectations and then provides the supplier with support to enable the supplier to become a leader in its industry. A good example is the sound relationship that existed between Xerox and Ames Rubber Corporation (Wendel 1995). Ames implemented the Xerox Quality model and improved productivity and delivery performance as well as seeing a tremendous decrease in its defect rate—from more than 30,000 parts per million to less than 10 ppm. In 1993, Ames became the recipient of the Malcolm Baldrige National Quality Award. Using the same Xerox Quality model, Trident Precision Manufacturing, another Xerox supplier, achieved the 1996 Malcolm Baldrige National Quality Award. These achievements of Ames and Trident represent the outstanding influence a large leading-edge company can have on its suppliers. As a leader of excellence, Xerox won the 1986 and 1997 Malcolm Baldrige National Quality Award.

In terms of education and training, when a customer, like Xerox, trains a supplier and the supplier implements the training, the supplier and customer benefit. This benefit results from all interested parties operating from the same viewpoint. Also, a positive ripple effect occurs when the supplier in-turn trains its own tier suppliers.

Rating Process

A rating process is useful to establish when a sound relationship exists. Both customer and supplier should establish their rating. Discussion can then be held to resolve differences and progress to a sound relationship. Relationship levels are defined as *beginner, intermediate, and sound.* Characteristics are scored with the point allocations of Table 2.5. (Norausky 1995). A beginner's score would be in the range of 150 to 249 total points; intermediate's score would be in the range of 250 to 549 total points and sound's score would be in the range of 550 and above (1000 maximum) and *with at least a 40 percent threshold of points for each characteristic.* Scoring is done by key people in both the customer and supplier organizations. Differences are then discussed and, as appropriate, an action plan defined.

Table 2.5. Scoring of characteristics.

Characteristic	Maximum Points
Trust	300
Communication	200
Commitment	200
Strategic planning	100
Prevention	100
Co-operation	100

Table 2.6. Trust scoring (300 points).

Scoring Factors	Customer	Supplier
Keeps promises (150 points)	x	x
Education and training (50 points)	x	x
Incoming inspection eliminated (50 points)	x	NA
Certification (50 points)	NA	x

Note: The "x" indicates to apply the scoring factor.

Unless the agreed upon total score falls within the sound level, a customer-supplier innovation team should not be formed.

Let's look at trust as an example. It is allocated 300 points. The rating factors for trust are shown in Table 2.6. In Table 2.6 there is a NA listing which means Not Applicable. The NA for elimination of incoming inspection is assigned since the customer must evaluate whether or not the supplier's product requires the customer to perform a level of incoming inspection. The objective is for the customer to perform no incoming inspection. The NA for certification places the burden of compliance on the supplier to achieve and remain in compliance for whatever certification that the customer may require, for example, ISO, QS, customer certification system.

Table 2.7. Trust scoring (example).

Scoring Factors	Customer	Supplier
Keeps promises (150 points)	112.5	37.5
Education and training (50 points)	40.0	45.0
Incoming inspection eliminated (50 points)	35.0	NA
Certification (50 points)	NA	40.0
Total	**187.5**	**122.5**

With the allocation of points for each of the scoring factors that the trust characteristic comprises, an assignment of degree of achievement can be used with the following:

- Keeps promises (150 points). This is rated as: none = 0%, some promises = 25%, most promises = 75% and all promises = 100 %.
- Education and training (50 points). This is rated as: none = 0%, some training = 25%, majority of training = 75% and all training = 100%.
- Incoming inspection eliminated (50 points). This is rated as: none = 100%, some inspection = 75%, majority of items inspected = 25% and all items inspected = 0%.
- Certification (50 points). This is rated as: none = 0%, meets some criteria = 25%, meets majority of criteria = 75% and meets all criteria = 100%.

A customer-supplier relationship example for the trust characteristic is shown in Table 2.7. Each relationship characteristic must be evaluated on its own merits. As a guide, *only for the trust scoring factors, at least 60 percent of the total points are needed for each factor in order to qualify for the sound relationship level.* In Table 2.7's example, supplier fails to meet the 60 percent threshold for *keeps promises.* Certainly, this suggests that the customer and supplier determine the root cause for the low score and then define and implement a corrective action plan.

Table 2.8. Communication scoring (200 points).

Scoring Factors	Customer	Supplier
Communication lines all levels. (50 points)	x	x
Issues: Price, service, quality, delivery addressed and negotiated up front. (50 points)	x	x
Immediate response to requests. (50 points)	x	x
Action meets requirements. (50 points)	x	x

Note: The "x" indicates to apply scoring factor.

The factors for scoring communication, commitment, strategic planning, prevention, and cooperation constitute the characteristics for a sound customer and supplier relationship. Tables 2.8 through 2.12 show these characteristics and describe the rating process.

Table 2.8 indicates the scoring factors for communication.

Assignment for the degree of achievement supporting Table 2.8 can be used as follows:

- Communication lines all levels (50 points). This is rated as: none = 0%, some = 25%, considerable = 75%, and entirely satisfactory = 100%.

- Issues: addressed and negotiated up-front (50 points). This is rated as: does not occur = 0%, some = 25%, majority = 75%, and fully = 100%.

- Response (50 points). This is rated as: none = 0%, occasional = 25%, majority = 75%, and always = 100%.

- Action meets requirements (50 points). This is rated as: never = 0%, sometimes = 25%, generally = 75%, and always = 100%.

Table 2.9 illustrates the scoring factors for commitment.

Assignment for the degree of achievement supporting Table 2.9 can be used as follows:

Table 2.9. Commitment (200 points).

Scoring Factors	Customer	Supplier
Customer committed to long-term business and volume with supplier. (25 points)	x	NA
Supplier committed to cost-effective production or service. (25 points)	NA	x
Both committed to make the other successful. (50 points)	x	x
Both committed to continuous improvement. (50 points)	x	x
Both engage in concurrent engineering. (50 points)	x	x

Note: The "x" indicates to apply scoring factor. NA = Not Applicable.

- Customer long-term business. (25 points) This is rated as: none = 0%, some = 25%, considerable = 75%, and fully = 100%.
- Supplier cost-effective production. (25 points) This is rated as: none = 0%, partial = 25%, considerable = 75%, and fully = 100%.
- Make each other successful. (25 points) This is rated as: no interest = 0%, little = 25%, considerable = 75%, and fully = 100%.
- Continuous improvement. (25 points) This is rated as: none = 0%, some = 25%, considerable = 75%, and fully = 100%.
- Concurrent engineering. (25 points) This is rated as: none = 0%, some = 25%, considerable = 75%, and fully = 100%.

Table 2.10 illustrates the scoring factors for strategic planning. Assignment for the degree of achievement supporting Table 2.10 can be used as follows:

- Joint planning sessions. (50 points) This is rated as: none = 0%, some = 25%, considerable = 75%, and fully = 100%.
- Operational plans. (25 points) This is rated as: none = 0%, some = 25%, considerable = 75 %, and fully = 100%.

Table 2.10. Strategic planning (100 points).

Scoring Factors	Customer	Supplier
Conduct joint strategic planning sessions. (50 points)	x	x
Define operational plans. (25 points)	x	x
Identify long-range plans, equipment or services to meet strategic objectives. (25 points)	x	x

Note: The "x" indicates to apply scoring factor.

Table 2.11. Prevention (100 points).

Scoring Factors	Customer	Supplier
Supplier uses preventive methods and techniques to avoid quality performance, delivery, and cost problems. (40 points)	NA	x
Customer uses a specification process compatible with supplier. (40 points)	x	NA
Lessons learned are shared throughout both organizations.	x	x
Both recognize and improve preventative measures taken by employees. (20 points)		

Note: The "x" indicates to apply scoring factor. NA = Not Applicable.

- Items to meet strategic objectives. (25 points) This is rated as: none = 0%, some = 25%, considerable = 75%, and fully = 100%.

Table 2.11 illustrates the scoring factors for prevention.
Assignment for the degree of achievement supporting Table 2.11 can be used as follows:

- Supplier preventive methods and techniques. (40 points) This is rated as: none = 0%, some = 25%, considerable = 75%, and fully = 100%.

Table 2.12. Cooperation (100 points).

Scoring Factors	Customer	Supplier
Identify risks and agree on handling risks and sharing consequences. (50 points)	x	x
Willingness to make each other successful. (50 points)	x	x

Note: The "x" indicates to apply scoring factor.

Table 2.13. Relationship scoring (example).

Characteristic		Customer	Supplier
Trust (300 points)		187.5	122.5
Commitment (200 points)		150.0	112.5
Communication (100 points)		120.0	100.0
Strategic planning (100 points)		60.0	55.0
Prevention (100 points)		75.0	80.0
Cooperation (100 points)		60.0	85.0
	Total	**652.5**	**555.0**

- Customer specifications. (40 points) This is rated as: none = 0%, some = 25%, considerable = 75%, and fully = 100%.
- Lessons learned sharing. (20 points) This is rated as: none = 0%, sometimes = 25%, frequently = 75%, and always = 100%.

Table 2.12 illustrates the scoring factors for cooperation.
Assignment for the degree of achievement supporting Table 2.12 can be used as follows:

- Risks. (50 points) This is rated as: never = 0%, sometimes = 25%, frequently = 75%, and always = 100%.
- Willingness to make each other successful. (50 points) This is rated as: never = 0%, sometimes = 25%, frequently = 75%, and always = 100%.

A complete example of relationship scoring is shown in Table 2.13. According to the guidance both the customer and supplier met the requirements for a sound relationship because:

1. the total score exceeded 550 points, 2. a minimum of 40 percent of the characteristic points were achieved and 3. 60 percent of the points for each of the trust items were achieved. However, the supplier only did so by 5 points for the total score. The customer and supplier need to reconcile the gap differences before proceeding with a customer-supplier innovation team arrangement.

The preceding treatment of the characteristics that constitute a sound relationship for a customer and supplier illustrate the process that is used to establish the baseline for moving into the area for a customer-supplier innovation team. The reader is encouraged to follow the rigor for the process to establish the type of relationship that exists. A worksheet is provided in Appendix B.2. The data and information obtained from this process enables both customer and supplier to more consistently identify and close gaps that may inhibit their relationship.

LESSONS LEARNED

1. A needs alignment for both customer and supplier provides insight on changes required to achieve a focused relationship. Both parties need to work at the alignment identification and resolve differences. It isn't a self-correcting process.

2. A supplier can take a partnership role in working with a customer. However, unless the customer recognizes this role on the part of the supplier, the full benefits will not be realized.

3. Without a sound customer-supplier relationship, attempts to establish a customer-supplier innovation team will be less effective than expected.

4. Trust is a keystone in the customer-supplier relationship. Trust should be based on facts and not emotion or some other type of *feel good* indicator. The supplier is either competent or not.

5. The trust journey maturity model provides a basis for understanding the state of the trust relationship and offers a more factual basis for determining whether to continue a relationship with a supplier. A sound relationship today may be a weak one tomorrow due to changes in either a supplier's or customer's infrastructure. Customer and supplier need to be alert for such changes in order to avoid a false sense of security in dealing with each other.

6. The method used to determine a sound customer-supplier relationship is predicated on facts that support the scoring process. Both customer and supplier must *stand back* from the scores and apply common sense to interpret the results. Common sense supported by open and continuous communication between customer and supplier set the stage for improvement.

7. The scoring model offers excellent insight into the perception of how the customer and supplier view their participation. Open dialogue will resolve differences.

SUMMARY

1. Customer and supplier needs, when aligned, provide the basis for the relationship to progress. Customer and supplier are encouraged to either use or create a table similar to Table 2.1. Realistic discussion about differences can then occur and actions defined to resolve these differences.

2. Customer and supplier roles are changing. Suppliers are operating as partners rather than followers. Customers are listening to suppliers. Business risks are being shared.

3. A sound customer-supplier relationship is advised before proceeding to define and operate a customer-supplier innovation team. Trust represents the keystone for a sound relationship. A trust process and maturity model provides guidance to determine the level of trust that exists in a relationship.

4. Levels of Maturity for a supplier relationship are covered in Table 2.2. The items listed provide a system perspective. It is noted that a primary/top supplier can be at a beginner level because the supplier possesses little or no track record.

5. Both customer and supplier should establish their relationship rating. Discussion can then be held to resolve differences and progress to a sound relationship. A rating process is used to score factors on the basis of 1000 points. Both parties require a total score of at least 550 points with a 40 percent minimum threshold of points for each characteristic and 60 percent minimum for each of the trust characteristic items in order to be considered as operating at a sound relationship. The score should not be considered as an absolute, but rather an indicator for resolution of any differences. The process enables both parties to hold discussions on a more factual basis and to be more realistic in discussing differences.

6. Lessons learned regarding customer-supplier relationships are shared.

7. The reader is presented with a series of questions regarding customer-supplier relationships.

QUESTIONS

Questions are intended to stimulate the reader's thinking about material in the chapter and necessary actions for transformation to the reader's organization.

1. What level of relationship alignment exists? Why?
2. Why is a change in the relationship needed?
3. What is the difficulty in changing?
4. What is the impact of not changing?
5. What is the assessment tool for determining level of the relationship?
6. What is done with the findings?
7. What is the role of senior management/role of employees in the customer-supplier relationship?
8. Does the customer-supplier relationship apply to all industries and operations?
9. Who is the customer? What is the role of the customer?
10. Who is the supplier? What is the role of the supplier?
11. What is the definition of a customer-supplier relationship?
12. How long will the relationship last? (Especially in a high-technology industry).
13. What is to be learned by each party from the relationship?
14. What is the competition doing relative to customer-supplier relationships?
15. What are the requirements of the user of the output from the customer-supplier relationship?
16. How is the relationship maintained once it becomes sound?
17. Why is a sound relationship necessary for an innovation team to be successful?
18. What are the elements that define a sound relationship?

19. Can you tell a relationship exists just by external signs? (handshake, smile).

20. What are the risks of not having a solid relationship and setting up a customer-supplier innovation team?

21. What are the economic benefits of the customer-supplier relationship? Market? Technical? Manufacturing? End user?

22. What are the consequences of not having the customer-supplier innovation team?

23. Why is the customer-supplier strategic vision and planning important?

24. Why hasn't the customer-supplier relationship been highlighted until now?

25. In rapidly changing technologies—can a customer-supplier relationship be sound? If not, why not?

26. What can be done about customer-supplier innovation teams where the time span is very short?

27. Why is it necessary to change the rules of engagement? And do what?

28. What are the needs of the customer?

29. What are the needs of the supplier?

30. What companies are considered best-in-class with customer-supplier innovation teams?

31. What is the rate of companies adopting the customer-supplier innovation team approach?

32. Can the customer-supplier relationship stand negative swings in the economy?

33. What are the key factors that define the relationship? Are these factors universal? Do these factors apply to large as well as small companies? Do these factors apply across sectors and industries?

34. What are the legal ramifications of the customer-supplier innovation team?

35. Can the customer-supplier innovation team include a sub-supplier to the prime supplier?

36. What are examples of companies with customer-supplier relationships?

37. What benefit enticements should a customer use to get the supplier to enter into a relationship? Are they effective?

38. What happens to the relationship when there is a change in leadership at either the customer and/or supplier end?

39. How is the relationship made to last?

40. Does a customer-supplier innovation team only apply to an external relationship? Can it apply to an internal relationship?

Finding the Right Talent

"The man that hath no music in himself.
Nor is not mov'd with concord of sweet sounds,
Is fit for treasons, strateagems, and spoils;
The motions of his spirits are dull as night,
And his affections dark as Erebus:
Let no such man be trusted. . . ."

Lorenzo in *The Merchant of Venice*

SO MANY PEOPLE, SO FEW CHOICES

There are 6 billion people in the world and 273 million in the United States (International Programs Center 1999). Population continues to increase as does the great mass of humanity. In civilized societies, people are educated at various levels. From a global perspective, a considerable choice exists in finding the right person to fill a job. However, what you see is not necessarily what you get especially when it comes to choosing the right person for whatever the job. Sure there are different screening techniques, but reality suggests that the true worth of an individual becomes evident under the pressure to produce a result.

Going from the population of the world to the situation where individuals are chosen from a company's population doesn't suggest that screening techniques are not effective. As Lee Iacocca said "You have to work with the cards that are dealt to you" (Iacocca 1984). With reference to people, this doesn't mean that you just indiscriminately assign people to jobs. You make the assignments in the most intelligent manner possible. Also, if the people are not the right people; change the rules and find people who can best perform the job and its responsibilities.

Working Group and Team

Before we proceed further in this chapter, it is appropriate to look at the differences between a working group and team. After all, declaring people a *team* does not automatically make one. The word *team* conveys different meanings to different people. In many situations, people tend to use the words *team* and *working group* interchangeably. The distinction between these words needs to be clarified before beginning a discussion about customer-supplier innovation teams.

"A *working group's* members meet to work on achieving set objectives usually defined by a group leader. Prioritized agendas ensure the efficient use of a member's time. Members share information or most effective practices and in most cases, performance of the group is accomplished by the members doing their respective jobs well. However, members do not take responsibility for results other than their own contribution." (Katzenbach and Smith 1994).

"A *team* is a small number of people with complementary skills who are committed to a common purpose, performance goals, and approach for which they hold themselves mutually accountable." (Katzenbach and Smith 1994). Thus, a major difference between a working group and a team is related to the distinction that team members require both individual and mutual accountability.

Getting Started

Over the years, many of us have encountered the situation where a working group or team needed to be formed and members identified. When managers were asked to identify members, in most cases, the individuals weren't the best choice because of any number of reasons. This situation is intolerable when it comes to members for the customer-supplier innovation team. Only the very best people must be identified as candidates to best ensure the team's success.

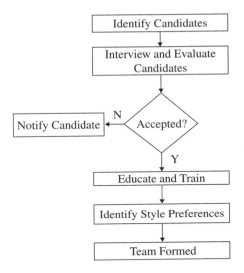

Figure 3.1. Team selection process.

Elements of the selection process for innovation team members involve: identification, interest, competency, interpersonal skills, communication skills, curiosity, ability to engage in a constant change process, system and process thinker, and passion to succeed as an individual and as a team member. A flow diagram for the selection process is shown in Figure 3.1. This chapter addresses all the steps in this flow diagram with the exception of team formation, which is covered in chapter 4.

TEAM SELECTION PROCESS

Identification

The sponsors (customer and supplier) are responsible for the team selection process. A flow diagram is shown in Figure 3.1. It stands to reason that before starting the selection process, the team's charter is clearly defined and agreed to by the sponsors. This charter includes: purpose, problem/situation, resources, number of team members from customer and supplier, general operational guidelines, co-leader responsibilities and authority, expected results, and end date for completion of the project. A worksheet and example are provided in Appendix C.1 and C.2.

Candidate Selection Criteria

1. Interest
2. Competency
3. Interpersonal skills
4. Communication skills
5. Curiosity
6. Change practitioner
7. System and process thinker
8. Passion to succeed as an individual
   and team member.

Figure 3.2.   Candidate selection criteria.

The process begins with the step to identify candidates. Sponsors review the knowledge and skills listed in the team's charter and then define a list of candidates. Sponsors discuss these candidates and reach agreement on which candidates to interview. Each sponsor informs their candidates of the problem/situation that needs to be solved and that they are being considered as a team member. The selection process is explained.

Sponsors define the criteria for candidate acceptance prior to holding interviews. Usually, these criteria are unique for a given team charter. However, a general listing of criteria is shown in Figure 3.2. A worksheet is provided in Appendix C.3.

General guidance about the criteria elements is as follows:

1. **Interest**—Obviously, the candidate must be interested in the project. This interest should be expressed by the candidate in terms of why the candidate is interested and why the candidate believes he or she can make a contribution. The candidate should be excited by the project's challenge.

2. **Competency**—The candidate's record of work successes should be outstanding. The extent that the candidate

encountered complex situations and provided innovative solutions is considered. The candidate should be encouraged to describe how a complex problem/situation was resolved. The candidate should explain actions he or she is taking to remain competent in the field.

3. **Interpersonal Skills**—The candidate must be able to listen and describe situations where he or she was involved in a conflict and the approach he or she took to obtain resolution. The candidate needs to explain why he or she possesses good interpersonal skills.

4. **Communication Skills**—The candidate must be able to engage in effective one-on-one conversations as well as presentation at meetings. The candidate should describe how he or she engages in a one-on-one conversation. The candidate should provide evidence of making effective presentations at meetings. Sponsors should evaluate a candidate's written reports for writing skill and competency of thought.

5. **Curiosity**—A candidate must exhibit a very high level of curiosity. The candidate should give examples that demonstrate his or her curiosity and the results of this curiosity.

6. **Change Practitioner**—The candidate possesses a record of engaging the change process and being successful with the change process. The extent that the candidate is a *risk taker* needs to be established. Also, the candidate needs to explain the process he or she uses to engage other people and organizations in the change process.

7. **System and Process Thinker**—The candidate must provide evidence of thinking in terms of systems and processes. The candidate discusses examples of system and process thinking and the results produced from such thinking.

8. **Passion to Succeed**—The candidate must exhibit evidence that he or she has passion to succeed as both an individual and team member. The candidate must explain why this isn't a contradiction and how he or she would operate to ensure both conditions could be satisfied.

Interview and Evaluate

Sponsors jointly conduct interview sessions. Outcomes of the interviews are evaluated. Candidates not selected are informed in a manner that indicates to each candidate their strengths and areas for improvement. This is a critical step since candidates not selected must understand the reason(s) for not being selected and be motivated to improve.

Acceptance

Sponsors hold an announcement meeting with the team members selected for the project. This represents an excellent opportunity for the sponsors to motivate the team relative to the importance of the project and their role. Also, an announcement is made concerning the appointment of the team's co-leaders. Co-leaders are used when the supplier is external to the customer. When both the supplier and customer are from the same company, it may then be more appropriate to appoint a leader.

Educate and Train

Team preparation is now necessary. The team jointly takes courses on creativity, innovation, conflict resolution, problem solving, basic economics, team operation, and diversity. These courses are designed for interaction of team members. Situations expected to be encountered during the project are interspersed in the course material. This starts the process for members to begin working together.

STYLE PREFERENCES

Team members take both the Myers-Briggs Type Indicator® Inventory, (MBTI)® (Consulting Psychologists Press, Inc. 1999), and the Kirton Adaption-Innovation (KAI) Inventory (Kirton 1999) instruments. This enables team members to better understand their own thinking and style preferences and those of other team members, Figure 3.3. A general discussion of the Myers-Briggs Type Indicator® Inventory, (MBTI)® and the Kirton Adaptation-Innovation (KAI) Inventory instruments will be covered in the following paragraphs to give the reader a basic understand-

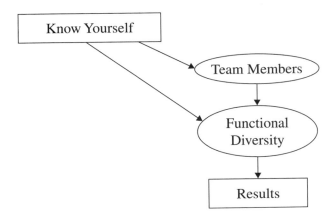

Figure 3.3. Key strength.

ing of these instruments. It is suggested that the reader attend a workshop or use a psychologist who is authorized to administer these instruments.

The style preference identification is intended to create an inspired team that is functionally diverse yet the members respect and support each other in striving to reach a common objective. "Take the case of General Motors versus Toyota. On a one-for-one comparative basis, individuals are generally matched. However, Toyota automobile models consistently occupy the top positions relative to quality and cost. Toyota has inspired teams of people. Inspired teams beat collections of individuals" (Meredith 1997). Even in sports, a baseball club with the best individuals doesn't always have the best team—so goes the Oakland Athletics when they lost the World Series in 1988 to the Los Angeles Dodgers and to the Cincinnati Reds in 1990. Todd Benzinger, a Reds player, said: "The A's have the best talent in baseball, we have the best team" (Townsend and Gebhardt 1992).

MYERS-BRIGGS TYPE INDICATOR® INVENTORY (MBTI)®

Introduction

According to NASA Headquarters (NASA 1994), team success in large part depends on its members' ability to interact with each other because of the myriad of different personalities involved.

Personality assessment tests can be interpreted incorrectly, but those such as the Myers-Briggs Type Indicator® Inventory (MBTI)® do at least allow individuals to learn something about themselves and how a variety of personality types interact. Team members may not be able to or even want to change their personality traits, but learning how to deal with others is an essential part of being an effective innovative team member.

Jung's Work: The Genesis for Myers-Briggs Type Indicator® Inventory (MBTI)®

Personality typing represents a method for self-discovery of a person's style preference. The research of Carl Jung is the foundation for style typing. (Jung 1971). He developed the theory that an individual belongs to a psychological type. He believed that there were two basic functions which people used: how information is perceived and how decisions are made. Jung believed that within these two functions, there were, in turn, two opposite ways of operating. A person can perceive information from: 1. his or her senses, or 2. his or her intuition. A person can make decisions based on: 1. objective logic, or 2. subjective feelings. Jung believed that each individual uses the different choices of operating with a varying amount of success and frequency. He believed that an order of preference could be identified for these choices within individuals. The choice which an individual uses most frequently represents his or her *dominant* choice. An auxiliary (2nd) choice, tertiary (3rd) choice, and inferior (4th) choice support the dominant choice. He asserted that each individual is either *extraverted* or *introverted* in his or her dominant choice. Jung believed that the dominant choice was so important, that it overshadowed all of the other choices in terms of defining personality type. Jung defined eight personality types as listed in Figure 3.4.

　　Katharine C. Briggs and her daughter Isabel Briggs-Myers further developed Jung's well-known work on personality typing. Actually, Isabel Briggs-Myers completed the work on Personality Types and made this theory popular. She demonstrated the importance of the supporting choice working with the dominant choice. Also, Isabel discovered that Jung overlooked the impor-

Jung's Personality Types

1. Extraverted sensing
2. Introverted sensing
3. Extraverted intuition
4. Introverted intuition
5. Extraverted thinking
6. Introverted thinking
7. Extraverted feeling
8. Introverted feeling

Figure 3.4. Jung's personality types.

tance of *judging* and *perceiving* as additional preferences. Currently, the theory states that every individual uses a primary mode to operate within four categories, Figure 3.5. The preference for each category is shown in Figure 3.6.

Usually, an individual finds that one mode of operation within a category is used more easily and frequently than the other modes. In other words, an individual prefers one mode over the other. When one mode is chosen for each of the preferences, the individual defines his or her personality type. In reality, individuals operate across the entire range of preferences with a normal and natural preference for a specific choice.

Flow of Energy addresses the manner which an individual receives his or her stimulation. Is it from within the individual (Introverted) or an external source (Extraverted)? What is the dominant choice?

Receiving and Process Information concerns an individual's preference in receiving and processing information. Does an individual trust his or her five senses (Sensing) to receive information, or does an individual rely on his or her instincts (Intuitive)?

Operational Categories

1. Flow of energy
2. Receiving and processing information
3. Manner of preference in making decisions
4. Basic daily life style

Figure 3.5. Operation categories.

Preferences

1. Extraverted or Introverted
2. Sensing or Intuitive
3. Thinking or Feeling
4. Judging or Perceiving

Figure 3.6. Preferences.

Make Decisions relates to whether an individual prefers to make his or her decisions based on logic and objective consideration (Thinking), or based on a subjective value system (Feeling).

Daily Life Style includes whether an individual is organized and purposeful, and more comfortable with scheduled, structured environments (Judging), or flexible and diverse, and more comfortable with open, casual environments (Perceiving).

Myers-Briggs Type Indicator® Inventory (MBTI)® Today

Currently, the Myers-Briggs Type Indicator® Inventory (MBTI)® represents the most widely known Personality Type instrument. Sixteen different Personality Types can be formed from the basic preferences. The characteristics frequently associated with each type are summarized in Table 3.1.

KIRTON ADAPTION-INNOVATION (KAI) INVENTORY

Background

Over three decades ago, Michael Kirton, a British psychologist, observed that people prefer to solve problems differently. One significant influence on his work was the conclusion, from his earlier study on management initiative, which showed that cognitive styles (attendant differences in personality) influenced the progress and success of corporate initiatives. Other important aspects of this work are the assumptions that creativity is part of problem solving, some of which may be judged creative, some not, and that as all people are problem solvers; therefore, all people are creative, to a greater or lesser extent, and in different styles. While managers were indicating their belief in the need for change, their willingness to support and embark in a specific change seemed dependent on how closely the change was related to their own characteristic style. Consequently, some changes were made quickly with little or no discussion, while other changes took years between the time the issue came up to the time the change was implemented. From this original study, Michael Kirton developed his theory about the difference in problem-solving styles and designed an instrument to measure these styles. According to the theory, everyone can be located on a continuum ranging from highly adaptive to highly innovative and the general population approaches the normal curve distribution (Norausky 1999A).

Theory

The Adaptor-Innovator Theory postulates that people have a preferred style for dealing with change, solving problems, making decisions, and using their creativity. The theory makes a crucial

Table 3.1. Characteristics frequently associated with each type.

Sensing Types

ISTJ Quiet, serious, earn success by thoroughness and dependability. Practical, matter-of-fact, realistic, and responsible. Decide logically what should be done and work toward it steadily, regardless of distractions. Takes pleasure in making everything orderly and organized—their work, their home, their life. Value traditions and loyalty.	**ISFJ** Quiet, friendly, responsible, and conscientious. Committed and steady in meeting their obligations. Thorough, painstaking, and accurate. Loyal, considerate, notice and remember specifics about people who are important to them, concerned with how others feel. Strive to create an orderly and harmonious environment at work and at home.
ISTP Tolerant and flexible, quiet observers until a problem appears, then act quickly to find workable solutions. Analyze what makes things work and readily get through large amounts of data to isolate the core of practical problems. Interested in cause and effect, organize facts using logical principles, value efficiency.	**ISFP** Quiet, friendly, sensitive, and kind. Enjoy the present moment, what's going on around them. Like to have their own space and to work within their own time frame. Loyal and committed to their values and to people who are important to them. Dislike disagreements and conflicts, do not force their opinions or values on others.

Introverts

Sensing Types

ESTP	ESFP
Flexible and tolerant, they take a pragmatic approach focused on immediate results. Theories and conceptual explanations bore them—they want to act energetically to solve the problem. Focus on the here-and-now, spontaneous, enjoy each moment that they can be active with others. Enjoy material comforts and style. Learn best through doing.	Outgoing, friendly, and accepting. Exuberant lovers of life, people, and material comforts. Enjoy working with others to make things happen. Bring common sense and a realistic approach to their work, and make work fun. Flexible and spontaneous, adapt readily to new people and environments. Learn best by trying a new skill with other people.
ESTJ	**ESFJ**
Practical, realistic, matter-of-fact. Decisive, quickly move to implement decisions. Organize projects and people to get things done, focus on getting results in the most efficient way possible. Take care of routine details. Have a clear set of logical standards, systematically follow them and want others to do also. Forceful in implementing their plans.	Warmhearted, conscientious, and cooperative. Want harmony in their environment, work with determination to establish it. Like to work with others to complete tasks accurately and on time. Loyal, follow through even in small matters. Notice what others need in their day-by-day lives and try to provide it. Want to be appreciated for who they are and for what they contribute.

Extraverts

Continued

Table 3.1. *Continued*

Intuitive Types

	INFJ	INTJ
	Seek meaning and connection in ideas, relationships, and material possessions. Want to understand what motivates people and are insightful about others. Conscientious and committed to their firm values. Develop a clear vision about how best to serve the common good. Organized and decisive in implementing their vision.	Have original minds and great drive for implementing their ideas and achieving their goals. Quickly see patterns in external events and develop long-range explanatory perspectives. When committed, organize a job and carry it through. Skeptical and independent, have high standards of competence and performance—for themselves and others.
	INFP	**INTP**
Introverts	Idealistic, loyal to their values and to people who are important to them. Want an external life that is congruent with their values. Curious, quick to see possibilities, can be catalysts for implementing ideas. Seek to understand people and to help them fulfill their potential. Adaptable, flexible, and accepting unless a value is threatened.	Seek to develop logical explanations for everything that interests them. Theoretical and abstract, interested more in ideas than in social interaction. Quiet, contained, flexible, adaptable. Have unusual ability to focus in depth to solve problems in their area of interest. Skeptical, sometimes critical, always analytical.

Intuitive Types

ENFP	ENTP
Warmly enthusiastic and imaginative. See life as full of possibilities. Make connections between events and information very quickly, and confidently proceed based on the patterns they see. Want a lot of affirmation from others, and readily give appreciation and support. Spontaneous and flexible, often rely on their ability to improvise and their verbal fluency.	Quick, ingenious, stimulating, alert, and outspoken. Resourceful in solving new and challenging problems. Adept at generating conceptual possibilities and then analyzing them strategically. Good at reading other people. Bored by routine, will seldom do the same thing the same way, apt to turn to one new interest after another.
ENFJ	**ENTJ**
Warm, empathetic, responsive, and responsible. Highly attuned to the emotions, needs, and motivations of others. Find potential in everyone, want to help others fulfill their potential. May act as catalysts for individual and group growth. Loyal, responsive to praise and criticism. Sociable, facilitate others in a group, and provide inspiring leadership.	Frank, decisive, assume leadership readily. Quickly see illogical and inefficient procedures and policies, develop and implement comprehensive systems to solve organizational problems. Enjoy long-term planning and goal setting. Usually well informed, well read, enjoy expanding their knowledge and passing it on to others. Forceful in presenting their ideas.

Extraverts

distinction between the level or capacity of an individual for solving problems (how good they are) and his or her style (how they prefer to do it). The former is addressed by asking questions such as: How well? How much? or How good? whereas the latter can be addressed by the question: In what way? Further, more research showed that style and level are not correlated, that one is not an indicator of the other. The Kirton Adaption-Innovation (KAI) Inventory assesses the problem-solving style and it does not correlate with level measures (Norausky 1999A).

Structure

Everyday people make decisions, solve problems, and deal with change. What is interesting is that the approach is different for different people. Structure to some people is very important while others prefer less structure. Some people, when problem solving, prefer more of a given structure and need agreement by consensus with more of that structure than do others. Those who need less structure and need agreement by consensus to less of it, seek consensus after problem solving rather than before. They cannot work without structure or even too little of it. The distinction seems fine but is critical on producing the diversity of problem-solving style. For all problem solvers, structure is both enabling and limiting; without it there could be no policy, paradigm, ethics, classification, no language, or even coherent thought. With too much of it there could be no adequate amount or scope for change. Our greater or lesser need for structure has an impact on how we deal with problems and the types of solutions we generate. These style differences are normally distributed on a continuum ranging from highly adaptive (a preference for a relatively high degree of structure) to highly innovative (a preference for a relatively low degree of structure). Each style will look at the same structure from a different viewpoint: one as enabling, the other as restricting (Norausky 1999A).

KAI Inventory

The Kirton Adaption-Innovation (KAI) Inventory labels the ends of the continuum as it measures Adaptive Style and Innovative Style. Behavior descriptions are shown in Table 3.2. The KAI is a

Table 3.2. KAI behavior descriptions.

Adaptor	Innovator
• Characterized by precision, reliability, efficiency, methodology, prudence, discipline, conformity. • Concerned with resolving problems rather then finding them. • Seeks solutions to problems in tried and understood ways. • Reduces problems by improvement and greater efficiency. • Seen as sound, conforming, safe, dependable. • Challenges rules rarely, cautiously and usually when supported. • Produces a few relevant, sound, safe ideas for prompt implementation. • Is master of detail. • Tends to use rules to solve problems.	• Seen as undisciplined thinking tangentially, approaching tasks from different angles. • Discovers problems and their avenues of solution. • Queries problems' basic assumptions; manipulates problems. • Seen as unsound, impractical; often shocks his opposite. • Capable of detailed routine work for only short bursts. • Quick to delegate routine tasks. • Tends to take control in unstructured situations. • Often challenges rules, little respect for past customs. • Produces many ideas including those seen as irrelevant, unsound, exciting, "blue sky." • Tends to bend rules to solve problems.

Reproduced by special permission of Michael J. Kirton, Occupational Research Centre, 'Highlands', Gravel Path, Berkhamsted, Herts, HP42PQ, UK. Granted 1999.

psychometric instrument for measuring the Adaptor-Innovator problem solving style. The KAI is one of the most researched and best-validated instruments currently available. The inventory consists of a list of 32 items that ask respondents to indicate how easy or difficult they would find it over a long period of time to maintain a range of adaptive and innovative behaviors available. The KAI is on one side of one sheet, requiring simple responses to short items. The results range over 100 points, having a centrally placed mean; this is true for the U.S. and U.K. general population samples as well as KAIs that have been translated (and validated) into several foreign languages. Research shows that less than ten points between the scores of two people represents the *same* score; less that 20 points difference represents a *similar* score and is a difference comfortable for both people. At 20 points difference, problems of mutual understanding and collaboration begin to arise that get increasingly more difficult with every additional increase in the difference between them. This has important implications for problem solving in teams. The Adaption-Innovation theory is used to assist in the understanding and management of human diversity (Kirton 1976, 1994), (Norausky 1999A).

WHERE TO NEXT?

At this point, team members are ready to tackle the project. However, opportunities for the team to get to know one another outside the demands of the project is essential for the team building process. Some companies use an *Outward Bound* experience to help create and shape team bonding. Team members need to learn about, respect and trust each other. With insight from the Myers-Briggs Type Indicator® Inventory (MBTI)® and Kirton Adaption-Innovation (KAI) Inventory instruments, each team member will be better able to identify and interact with fellow team members. This process continues throughout the existence of the team. Team members will return to their former positions before the project in a state of career maturity. This offers a win-win situation for the team member and the sponsors.

LESSONS LEARNED

1. Sponsors must agree to the content of the team charter and candidate selection criteria.

2. The candidate interviewing process must be conducted in an informed manner on the part of the sponsors. Sponsors should run through a mock interview to better ensure unification of the interview process.

3. Candidates not selected must receive immediate counseling from the appropriate sponsor as to actions needed to be taken to improve the chance of securing future project opportunities.

4. Sponsors need to hold a meeting with the accepted candidates to explain the importance of the project and role of the team members.

5. Insight from the Myers-Briggs Type Indicator® Inventory (MBTI)® and Kirton Adaption-Innovation (KAI) Inventory instruments are not intended to *label* team members. The intent is for the team member to better understand his or her own preferences and those of the other team members. Sponsors are responsible to instruct team members on the value and use of these instruments before taking the instruments.

6. Team members must be given a bonding experience before starting the project. Otherwise, the ability for the team to work together on the project will be put at risk.

SUMMARY

1. The word *team* conveys different meanings to different people. The terms *team* and *working group* are used interchangeably. The difference between these terms is that team members require both individual and mutual accountability for the team's actions to either succeed or fail.

2. Project sponsors (customer and supplier) follow a team selection process to form an effective team. The sponsors define a team charter. Based on the charter, the sponsors better understand the type of individuals needed for the team and, therefore, can identify a list of candidates. A Team Charter Worksheet and example is provided in Appendix C.1 and C.2.

3. Interviewing and evaluating candidates is done against established criteria and a unique criteria is listed in the team charter. Sponsors conduct a mock interview to unify their approach to interviewing candidates. General criteria guidance is presented. Sponsors are cautioned to counsel those candidates not accepted in a manner to motivate these candidates for future opportunities. Sponsors hold a meeting with accepted candidates to reinforce the importance of the project and the role of the candidates. Also, this meeting is used to announce the appointment of the co-leaders for the team. A Candidate Selection Worksheet is provided in Appendix C.3.

4. Once selected, team members are trained jointly in courses involving: creativity, innovation, conflict resolution, problem solving, basic economics, team operation, and diversity. These courses are designed for interaction of team members.

5. Team members take the Myers-Briggs Type Indicator® Inventory (MBTI)® and the Kirton Adaption-Innovation (KAI) Inventory instruments. Results from these instruments provide team members with a better understanding of their

preferences and those of other team members. The intent is that through better understanding, improved team interaction will occur.

6. Team formation takes more that a declaration that a team now exists. Some companies use an *Outward Bound* experience to further bond team members into a positive working relationship.

7. Lessons learned regarding the process to identify, select, and accept team members for the customer-supplier innovation team are covered.

8. The reader is presented with a series of questions regarding the process to identify, select, and approve team members for the customer-supplier innovation team.

QUESTIONS

1. What people criteria should be considered for long-term projects?

2. What people criteria should be considered for short-term projects?

3. What is a *team?* What is a *work group?*

4. Does my organization use *work groups* or *teams?*

5. How effective are the *work groups* or *teams?*

6. What should be included in a team charter?

7. What is usually done in putting a team together?

8. What should be done in putting a team together?

9. What is the selection process for each team member?

10. Why is a proper selection process important?

11. What are the consequences of not having a proper selection process?

12. After a team member is selected—what then?

13. Do innovation teams work in small companies where there are a limited number of candidates? Explain.

14. How is the issue of diversity and competent candidates resolved for composition of the team especially when preference instruments and the innovation quotients are used?

15. How do you put an innovation team together?

16. What constitutes the selection model for team members?

17. What is the profile for an innovation team member?

18. How does identification and selection of an innovation team member differ from selecting a team member for another purpose?

19. What is the profile of the people doing the selection? Why are they qualified to do the selection?

20. What process is used to identify innovation team members?

21. What process is used when a candidate isn't selected?

22. What process is used when the person declines to be an innovation team member?

23. Is the identification process perfect? What are hidden problems?

24. Is the selection process perfect? What are hidden problems?

25. Do the identification and selection processes work for all size companies (small and large)? Are they industry specific?

26. What factors must be agreed to by the customer-supplier before the identification and selection processes begin?

27. What specific level of issue/problem exists to activate the identification and selection processes?

28. What filter is used for identification of potential candidates?

29. What is done to ensure a consistent identification process is used by the customer and supplier?

30. What happens when a team member decides to change companies and then leaves the team prior to the team meeting its objective?

31. What is the time frame to identify and select candidates? How is this achieved? How fast should the team be put together?

32. Are team members asked or told to participate?

33. Does a chemistry across team members have to exist?

34. What about a candidate's stamina and energy to work in a free but results-driven environment? How does this affect candidate selection and team success?

35. What education and training is needed on the part of the people making the identification/selection of team members?

36. Do the principles of high-performance work teams apply? If not, why not?

Determining Innovation Focus

"... the world offers itself to your imagination,
calls to you like the wild geese, harsh and exciting—
over and over announcing your place
in the family of things."

Mary Oliver, "Wild Geese"

INNOVATION FOCUS (IF)

This chapter on Innovation Focus enables sponsors (customer and supplier), team members, and the team to establish the extent that they support and/or prefer activities for innovation. As shown in Figure 4.1, IF is the next step in the path for a team member to expand the preference style process to the team and sponsors. The approach is needed in conjunction with the Myers-Briggs Type Indicator® Inventory (MBTI)® and Kirton Adaption-Innovation (KAI) Inventory instruments to bring a full dimensional representation about innovation levels concerning the team member, team, and sponsors. In particular, the IF discloses an organization's preference for innovation. This insight would not exist otherwise for comparative purposes. The IF scores for all parties provide preference data. This allows calculation of the Innovation Focus Quotient (IFQ) using the IF data from team members, the team, and sponsors. Standards are defined for specific quotients. Quotient values are then compared to standard values and action plans defined.

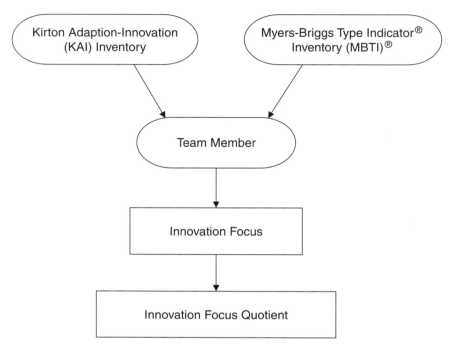

Figure 4.1.   Innovation preference.

Both small and large companies have used the IF and IFQ approach. These companies regard the IF and IFQ as tools for a competitive advantage.

The IF and IFQ are powerful tools. These tools provide a platform for relative discovery, comparison, and improvement. They support a higher level of understanding and agreement among team members, the team, and sponsors (Norausky 1995). This is an essential condition to spur breakthrough thinking for innovation results.

Over the past several years, it was noted that the majority of sponsors achieved innovation results but did not determine the extent that their culture was innovative. The reasoning was *we are producing innovation results; therefore, our culture must be innovative.* This type of reasoning does not guarantee that the culture will be innovative in the future especially when facing chaotic market conditions on a global scale. On this basis alone, the value for using an approach such as the IF and IFQ is warranted.

Self-Assessment for Innovation Focus (IF)

Each of the team members need to establish their interest and focus about innovation and the innovation process to better understand their own outlook and, thus, be better able to work with other team members in the innovation process. The following self-assessment instrument (Norausky 1995), Figure 4.2, is based on work with people in various worldwide operations.

Scoring

A score of 50 and above indicates an acceptable innovation focus for the team member. Thirty to 49 suggests that the person is in the developing stage for an innovation focus. Less than 29 indicates the person doesn't have an innovation focus and may not be a contributing member of the team.

Assessment of the Organization's Innovation Focus (IF)

Once an individual team member's interest and focus are established about innovation and the innovation process, the next step is to assess the organization's interest and focus. The organization's assessment (Norausky 1995), Figure 4.3, is completed by senior managers from both the customer and supplier answering the questions. The average score is calculated for both customer and supplier. Knowing the team member's self-assessment score and score of each organization enables a dialogue to be established between the customer and supplier team members. The objective is to reach an understanding of where improvements are needed in the use of innovation and the innovation process.

Scoring

A score of 50 and above indicates an acceptable IF for the organization. Thirty to 49 suggests that the organization is in the developing stage for an IF. Less than 29 indicates the organization doesn't have an IF and may need alignment for an innovation focus.

Instruction: Please circle the number that represents your answer to each question.

Completely Accurate
Between
Somewhat Accurate
Between
Not Accurate

1. I am curious about *why* things happen 0 1 2 3 4

2. I am always thinking of ways to apply new ideas to my job 0 1 2 3 4

3. People in my work group are interested in my ideas 0 1 2 3 4

4. I enjoy the challenge of making process changes 0 1 2 3 4

5. I look for the latest gadgets and how they might be of use to me 0 1 2 3 4

6. Being better than the competition because of innovative products, processes or systems is a driving source for my innovation 0 1 2 3 4

7. I find myself day-dreaming about new ways to make things better 0 1 2 3 4

8. I read publications relating to many diverse topics for ideas 0 1 2 3 4

9. I am aware that all of our key competitors are using innovation as a competitive advantage 0 1 2 3 4

Figure 4.2. Self-assessment: IF scoring.

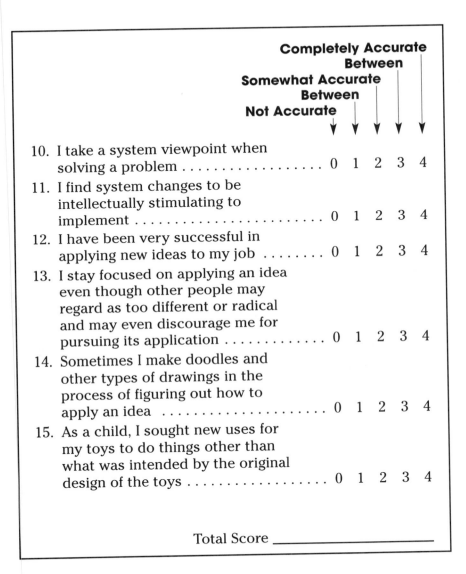

Completely Accurate
Between
Somewhat Accurate
Between
Not Accurate

10. I take a system viewpoint when
    solving a problem 0   1   2   3   4

11. I find system changes to be
    intellectually stimulating to
    implement 0   1   2   3   4

12. I have been very successful in
    applying new ideas to my job 0   1   2   3   4

13. I stay focused on applying an idea
    even though other people may
    regard as too different or radical
    and may even discourage me for
    pursuing its application 0   1   2   3   4

14. Sometimes I make doodles and
    other types of drawings in the
    process of figuring out how to
    apply an idea 0   1   2   3   4

15. As a child, I sought new uses for
    my toys to do things other than
    what was intended by the original
    design of the toys 0   1   2   3   4

Total Score _____

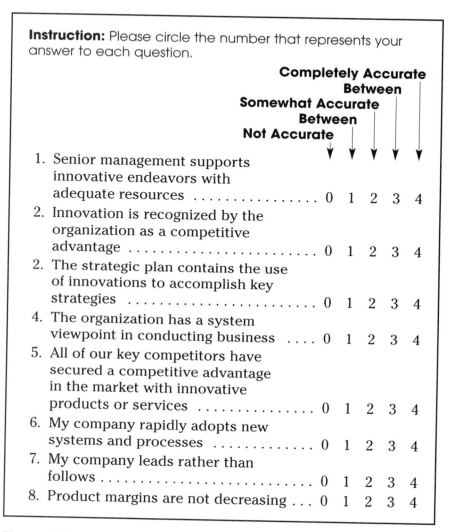

Figure 4.3.   Organization assessment: IF scoring.

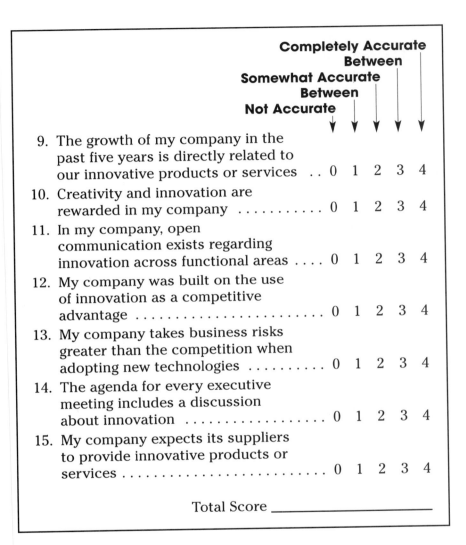

Completely Accurate
Between
Somewhat Accurate
Between
Not Accurate

9. The growth of my company in the
   past five years is directly related to
   our innovative products or services .. 0 1 2 3 4

10. Creativity and innovation are
    rewarded in my company 0 1 2 3 4

11. In my company, open
    communication exists regarding
    innovation across functional areas 0 1 2 3 4

12. My company was built on the use
    of innovation as a competitive
    advantage 0 1 2 3 4

13. My company takes business risks
    greater than the competition when
    adopting new technologies 0 1 2 3 4

14. The agenda for every executive
    meeting includes a discussion
    about innovation 0 1 2 3 4

15. My company expects its suppliers
    to provide innovative products or
    services 0 1 2 3 4

Total Score _____

INNOVATION FOCUS QUOTIENT (IFQ)

The IFQ (Norausky 1995) involves four entities: team member, team, customer, and supplier companies. The IFQ provides an indicator of the level that the innovation focus exists and enables actions to be identified and taken in order to achieve synchronization with the other entities. The greatest contribution of the IFQ is to provide everyone involved with the customer-supplier innovation team a basis to discuss differences and whether or not these differences require a change to be made.

The generic equation for the IFQ is defined as: ***IFQ = entity of interest divided by the comparative entity.*** Thus, Innovative Focus Quotients are expressed as:

IFQ_1 = Team Member's Innovation Focus ÷ Team Member's Company (Customer or Supplier) Innovation Focus.

IFQ_2 = Team Member's Innovation Focus ÷ Other Company's (Customer or Supplier) Innovation Focus.

IFQ_3 = Team Member's Innovation Focus ÷ Team's Innovation Focus.

IFQ_4 = Team's Innovation Focus ÷ Customer Innovation Focus.

IFQ_5 = Team's Innovation Focus ÷ Supplier Innovation Focus.

Innovation Focus Assessments for the four entities: team member, team, supplier, and customer are used to obtain a total score value for each entity. The customer and supplier scores represent an average value of senior management for each of these entities.

Total score values are used to calculate IFQ_1 through IFQ_5. The IFQ standard is covered in Table 4.1. The resulting IFQ values should not be less than one for IFQ_1, IFQ_2, IFQ_4 and IFQ_5. The reason is that the team and team members must have a strong innovation focus belief and commitment to bring success to the team's projects. The IFQ_3 value may range from less than one to greater than one. In the situation where IFQ_3 is 0.75 or less, this should be cause to understand why the team member's score is low and what is needed to raise the score. The customer and supplier selection board can then help the team member define and

Table 4.1. IFQ standard.

IFQ	Standard
IFQ_1	Not be less than one
IFQ_2	Not be less than one
IFQ_3	Range from 0.75 to greater than one.
IFQ_4	Not be less than one
IFQ_5	Not be less than one

Table 4.2. IF score (example).

Entity	IF Score
Team member	52
Team	54
Customer	53
Supplier	51

Table 4.3. Innovation focus quotient (example).

IFQ	Value	Comment
IFQ_1	52/53	Review
IFQ_2	52/51	Accept
IFQ_3	52/54	Accept
IFQ_4	54/53	Accept
IFQ_5	54/51	Accept

pursue an action plan to raise the team member's score. An IFQ example is shown in Table 4.3 based on Table 4.2.

In the Table 4.3 example, the IFQ_1 is listed as *review* because the value is less than one. This means that the team member's organization has a stronger preference for IF than the team member does. A discussion is advised to determine the reason(s). This does not mean that the team member should not participate on the team.

LESSONS LEARNED

1. Values obtained for the Innovation Focus (IF) and Innovation Focus Quotient (IFQ) are not absolute. These subjective values are intended to bring the preferences to the forefront and encourage open dialogue for improvement.

2. Team members with an IF score less than 29 should determine whether or not change is possible. Experience indicates that unless a change can be made, then it is best that the team member is not included on the team. If the person's expertise is vital, then this person can function as an advisor to the team. Also, the sponsors need to review their selection process to determine why the person was selected as team member.

3. The IF scores for the sponsors need to be at least 45 or better. Lower scores raise concerns that support for the innovative process may not be provided when needed.

4. The IF and IFQ process encourage dialogue and subsequent action plans for improvement. A win-win situation.

SUMMARY

1. The Innovation Focus (IF) and the Innovation Focus Quotient (IFQ) provide team members, the team, and sponsors with an understanding and agreement on the level of innovation preference. The IF and IFQ allows an expansion of the preference process to the team and sponsors. In particular, the IF discloses an organization's preference for innovation. This insight would not exist otherwise for comparative purposes.

2. An IF score less than 29 indicates a team member or sponsors do not have an IF and may need alignment for an innovation focus.

3. Standard values are designated for the various IFQ combinations.

4. Calculated IFQ values can be compared to the standard IFQ values.

5. The IF and IFQ create a process for dialogue among team members, the team and sponsors. Action can be defined, as needed.

6. Lessons learned regarding the process for the IF and IFQ are presented.

7. The reader is presented with a series of questions regarding the use of the IF and IFQ.

QUESTIONS

1. Why is an Innovation Focus (IF) necessary?

2. What processes are used to determine the IF for the team member, team, and sponsors?

3. How is an IF determined—individual, team, customer, supplier?

4. What happens if either and/or both customer and supplier do not have a satisfactory IF score but they want to form a customer-supplier innovation team?

5. What is the Innovation Focus Quotient (IFQ)? How is it calculated?

6. What is the basis of the IFQ?

7. Who uses the IF approach?

8. Does the IF change once it is determined?

9. Why is the IF approach needed since the Myers-Briggs Type Indicator® Inventory (MBTI)® and Kirton Adaption-Innovation (KAI) Inventory instruments are used?

10. Who is qualified to evaluate the IF outcome for the individual, team, and organization?

11. When the IF indicates unfavorable results what is done to bring the situation into positive alignment? Is such alignment needed?

12. What is the definition for IF?

13. How should the IF be applied?

14. What happens if a team member leaves and new members are added?

15. What happens if there is a change in the customer and/or supplier organization with regard to the IF?

Creativity and the Team

"The mind can only see what it is prepared to see."

Edward de Bono, *Serious Creativity*

"Man's mind, stretched to a new idea, never goes back to its original dimension."

Oliver Wendell Holmes

CREATIVITY—WHAT IS IT?

When was the last time you stood on your head? As a child? Teenager? Adult? Never! If you did, what do you remember about the experience? Being creative requires that a person unblock conventional practices in order to *see* new possibilities.

The right side of the brain contributes to creativity while the left side draws on logic. In the mid 1960s a high school teacher, Betty Edwards, wondered why some students could draw and others couldn't. She wanted to teach all her students to draw. She discovered that those students who couldn't draw could be taught to draw by tricking the *logic* of the mind by simply looking at the item to be drawn from a different perspective (Edwards 1987). For example, to draw some of the facial features of a person, the artist would not think in terms of cheeks, eyes, mouths, but would view and understand the face to be comprised of straight and curved lines. Once the mind accepted this idea, drawing became fun and a reasonable representation of a face could be drawn.

But you don't have to be an artist to be creative. If you examine the situations you face each day, you'll discover just how creative you are. For example, you might be out of toothpaste but substitute baking soda to clean your teeth. At work, the hard drive on your computer crashes. You use the computer of a colleague who is on vacation.

Creativity requires data and information. In a perfect world the data and information would be accurate and we would not have to do any thinking. Creativity requires thinking.

The biggest impediment to creativity is the resistance to not embarrass oneself. Creativity requires taking risks. You have to expose yourself as being a non-conformant. For example, a procurement manager is informed that an expected shipment of sheet stock will be delayed for two days. Production needs this stock because they are operating on a just-in-time mode. The procurement manager assumes the risk to find a creative solution. He simply thinks *where else could I get the stock in the required time?* He determines that another division has the needed sheet stock and is able to secure an adequate quantity for production to meet the time requirement.

What creative examples can you recall where you were creative during your workday? Keep a journal of your creative exploits and solutions. It will be fun and you'll be surprised how absolutely clever you are. A form is provided in Appendix D.1 for this purpose.

An individual or team can sit around and think up ideas. Certainly this is a feel good process. Creativity not only includes the act of thinking but also the necessity of putting the creativity into action. Action to bring an idea from plausibility to feasibility makes the creative inspiration come alive. It also involves risk. Risk of exposing oneself or the team to criticism especially if the idea represents a serious departure from previous conventional solutions.

So how should creativity be defined? There are many definitions of creativity. In fact, a search on the Internet yielded forty-nine definitions. One aspect of the definition that must be made clear is the confusion that some people seem to have with creativity and innovation. Generally, people tend to use the terms creativity and innovation as interchangeable. This is not correct as can be seen from these definitions:

Creativity is the process of generating ideas that may or may not have value for practical application.

Innovation is the process of applying ideas obtained from the creative process. They are implemented because of the significant value they offer to solve an existing problem or prevent a potential one.

Therefore, the difference relates to generating ideas compared to applying these ideas. Customer and supplier team members must realize this difference as they work to make changes that result in significant improvements and breakthroughs.

In the real world, a blur exists between the creative and innovative processes. The reason is based on the fact that these two processes must be combined to produce a *solution system,* Figure 5.1.

Creative Dependency

For the purpose of understanding the creative process, it must be considered separate from the innovative process. This same consideration applies to understanding the innovative process.

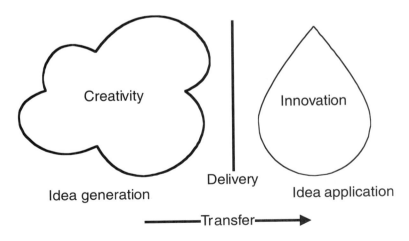

Figure 5.1. Solution system.

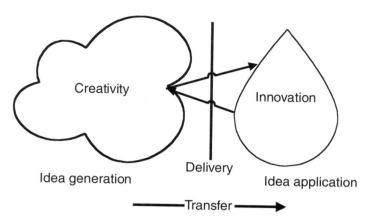

Figure 5.2. Process dependency.

To use the creative process, it is imperative that a strategic view is taken in that the best ideas, in fact, great ideas, only are valuable when implemented by the innovative process. Though a free wheeling spirit should and must exist to a large extent during the creative process, the point cannot be lost that a solution is required and implementation must be achieved. The diagram of forward and rearward vectors between creativity and innovation, Figure 5.2, addresses the reality of non-separation. If this reality becomes distorted, the creative-innovative system fails to meet its expectations.

The Creative Person

As mentioned previously, everyone possesses the potential to be creative. It is recognized that some people need more practice than others do. Creativity can be learned. It is a skill. If you can think, you can create!

There are three areas that should be satisfied for a person to be creative. 1. Usually, persons must possess knowledge in the field where they are seeking to find a creative solution. Normally, it would be unreasonable to expect a person not familiar with astrophysics to find a creative solution to a complex problem/ situation in astrophysics. 2. The person must understand and be able to apply skills of creative thinking to a given problem/

situation. 3. The person must be motivated to engage in the creative process at a level where discovery of the creative idea that becomes the solution for the problem/situation represents the reward (Amabile 1992).

Creative Process

The creative process is a fluid process. It conforms to no particular set of steps. The steps used by an individual or team are based on preference. Such preference may change for the same individual or team depending on conditions of problem complexity, importance, and time pressure to deliver ideas. The creative process is intended to produce ideas that offer solutions to solve problems and/or improve products, services, processes, or systems. Politics have no place in either the creative or innovative processes and neither does rank nor the participant's position. Equality of team members is essential for free exchange to occur. A creative process involves a variety of techniques, selection, and use. Creative techniques are covered later in this chapter.

The approach for a creative process should satisfy these conditions:

- Reason for the creativity—problem, issue, improvement
- Techniques to be used
- Idea evolution/building
- Evaluation of the ideas generated
- Accepted ideas as input to innovative process.

Successful use of a creative process suggests that team members participate according to the steps in Figure 5.3:

Relax—Do what makes you feel calm and without tension. This may include background influence, for example, music, color of the room, room lighting conditions, clothing you are wearing.

Clear the Mind—From a self-talk standpoint, tell yourself that you are going to lift out the blocks of thoughts that clutter your mind, for example, 1st block: concern about a bill, 2nd block: concern about a son or daughter, 3rd block: concern about a health issue. After removal of these blocks,

Creative Process Participation

1. Relax
2. Clear the mind
3. Focus
4. Encourage chaos
5. Connectivity and linkages

Figure 5.3. Creative process participation.

say to yourself, *Is there anything else?* If your self-talk *responds* with a *yes,* repeat the clearing process with different blocks that come to mind.

Focus—Begin by writing your name upside down and backward on a piece of paper for at least ten times. You are now ready to address the problem/solution from a creative standpoint. You can stand mentally outside of the traditional thinking. You are free to explore. Don't look back!

Encourage Chaos—This may appear like a contradiction because of the effort expended to relax, clear the mind, and focus but in reality what is being done is to create a swirl of mental activity and observe the flow of ideas. Usually, this observation sparks creative ideas.

Connectivity and Linkages—While participating in the creative process and proceeding to generate ideas, being able to think in terms of connecting ideas with other ideas provides a powerful means for evolving even better ideas. Here is an excellent example: for over 4000 years, glass was made by melting dry mineral ingredients. Making pure silica glass required melting the purest quartz at incredibly high temperatures. This was not a very cost-effective process. J. Franklin Hyde, a Corning Inc. organic chemist reasoned that silica existed in liquid chemicals as well as dry minerals. Why not extract silica from a liquid chemical? In a very simple demonstration, he squirted liquid silicon tetrachloride into the flame of an oxygen-acetylene torch. It reacted with the water vapor produced by the burning fuel to form an extremely pure glass-fused silica. Success was his! All because he made the connection that silica glass could come from a liquid as well as dry minerals. Today, fused silica glass is used for demanding applications, for example, *stepper* lens assemblies for photolithography to print circuits onto computer chips, space shuttle windows that withstand extreme thermal changes (Norausky 1999 B).

How Are Ideas Generated?

There is an apparent contradiction in that creativity is viewed as the spontaneous generation of ideas, yet techniques are used to bring structure to this process. Why is this so? Most people who are participating in the creative process are looking for a path that will lead them to rapid generation of ideas, for example, so many ideas in a given time frame. This thought is also brought on by the sponsors of a creative session since *the idea* may be required to solve a very expensive on-going problem, such as an oil well burning out of control. This is costing millions of dollars per day in lost revenue.

The seed of an idea or the whole idea is formed in the mind of one team member. When shared with other team members, this idea may be modified until a more refined idea emerges from the team. The diagram in Figure 5.4 depicts a flow diagram that illustrates the idea generation process.

Model Phases:
- **Preparation Phase**—For this phase: the problem, reason for the need to generate the idea, is explored to ensure that the team feels comfortable in understanding the basis for the need and the need itself. This is the questioning phase.
- **Formulation Phase**—Ideas are generated spontaneously according to accepted methods or techniques.
- **Enrichment Phase**—Original ideas are modified partially or completely. Ideas are more focused to meet requirements.
- **Selection Phase**—Ideas that emerge from the enrichment phase become candidates for selection.

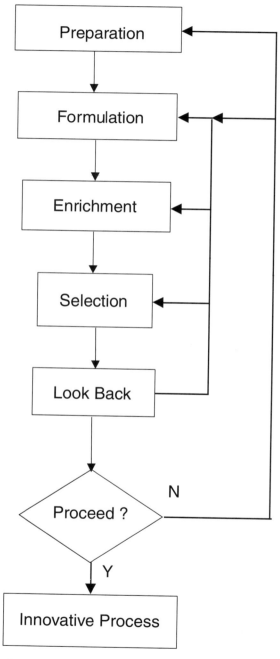

Figure 5.4. Creative idea generation process.

- **Look Back Phase**—Sometimes great ideas don't appear to be great during the initial phases. A look back process ensures that a *good* idea isn't missed. If a good idea was overlooked, the idea is processed through the enrichment and selection phases.

Recording Process

The recording process must ensure all data and information is captured. Guidance is as follows:

- A consistent process is used to record information and data concerning the idea. This includes the name of the originator.
- This brings up the issues of who becomes the recorder. In most cases, the recorder should not be a team member. When a team member is the scribe, this can mentally remove the team member from making the level of contribution expected of a team member in the idea-generation process. A few protocol points concerning the scribe: The scribe is not permitted to facilitate the idea-generation process. This task is the responsibility of a team member designated by the team, usually an outside person or a co-leader.
- A worksheet is provided in Appendix D.2. This worksheet provides a permanent and consistent record of information and data associated with the generation, discussion, selection, enrichment, and look back phases. It can be recorded in either traditional hard copy or electronic medium.
- With the use of laptop computers, usually the work sheet information and data are entered into the computer and projected onto a screen. The spontaneous generation of ideas can be captured in record form by the use of briefing pads and photographed with a digital camera for the record or even voice input.
- A consistent process used to capture all the information and data may detract from the creative process. Each team will adjust the recording process for its own comfort level without compromising the record of data and information.

- All team members should have access to the material that is generated. This can be accomplished with a network hook-up to the database. A member can retrieve from the database as required. If the team isn't afforded a computer and a computerized system, then the traditional bank of worksheets hung on the wall approach will suffice.

So when we address the topic of how ideas are generated, we must include the generation, recording, storage, and retrieval components in the answer to the question.

CREATIVE IDEA-GENERATING TECHNIQUES

Books, magazine articles, and technical papers flourish with theories and information about techniques to generate creative ideas. However, it's the experience with customer-supplier teams that reveals the use of the most common techniques. But a word of caution is warranted. Many factors associated with the culture and environment of the team determine the techniques that are used. When all is said and done, it's the team's choice on how to best generate creative ideas.

The concept of get ready, get set, go—start generating creative ideas—represents a popular notion about the creative idea generating process. Behind the scenes, a good deal of planning goes into preparation and selection of the technique(s) considered appropriate for a session to achieve a required outcome.

Customer-Supplier team: Common creative idea-generating techniques are listed in Table 5.1. As stated previously, many techniques are available but the comfort level of using a few proven techniques enables the team to focus on the idea-generating process rather than the techniques. Further, one or more techniques may be used to create an orchestrated process. A technique used to generate ideas should become transparent and not detracting from the process.

Notes on Stage*

First Stage is the beginning stage. Circumstances for ideas are better defined and many ideas are generated.

Second Stage is the interim stage where creative ideas exist. A discarding and building process occurs to provide a convergence for the generating additional ideas.

Table 5.1. Customer-Supplier team: Common creative idea generating techniques

Technique	Stage*	Application
Brainstorming	All three stages	Pure idea generation
Force analysis	Starts at the first stage; continues through other two stages	Identifies driving forces
TRIZ	Starts at the first stage; continues through other two stages	Idea generation, evolution, and breakthrough
Mind mapping	All three stages	Idea generation
Free association	All three stages	Stimulates the mind to conceive ideas and their linkages.

Third Stage is the final stage. Creative ideas are evaluated in terms of the objective. Ideas that emerge become the source to start the innovative process.

Brainstorming

Whenever people hear the words *you need to be creative,* they think immediately of brainstorming as the creative-thinking technique that will enable them to generate ideas. It is without a doubt the most popular and widely used technique. It was introduced in 1939 by Alex Osborn (Osborn 1979).

There are pros and cons.

Pros of a brainstorming session:

- Generates many ideas very quickly.
- Taps into ideas and views from diverse perspectives.
- Initial ideas often lead to other ideas both during and after a session.

Cons of a brainstorming session:

- Only produces ideas, not an action plan.

- Produces ideas that may or may not apply to the objective.
- Some participants may dominate while others are quieter.
- Participants usually jump into idea generation without prior preparation.
- Participants are not shown how to get novel ideas. This show of brilliance is just supposed to occur.

Brainstorming is a high energy, idea-producing technique. For brainstorming or for that matter all creative sessions to be effective, adherence to four basic rules are required. It is suggested that these rules be posted on the wall in the room of a session and given as handout material to participants. Also, a session leader should remind participants of these rules before the start of a session and, of course, as appropriate during a session.

Brainstorming Rules:
1. **Avoid criticism**—No matter what . . . every idea is encouraged and welcomed. Negative reactions both verbal and nonverbal are not to be exhibited by any participant. The tolerance is zero. No excuses!
2. **Free-wheel**—The wilder the idea, the better. It is easy to reduce an idea, if necessary, than to build-up an idea.
3. **Quantity**—The more ideas the better since the probability is greater that a few good ideas exist.
4. **Combine and improve**—Ideas trigger other ideas. Participants should look to build on a single idea or a combination of other participants' ideas. This combining and improving process should be shared with the other participants.

The prior material on brainstorming demonstrates serious shortcomings. In over 3000 brainstorming sessions, I have witnessed the attitude and behavior that brainstorming will generate the ideas we need. Let's just get the team together and start generating ideas. Wrong! By modifying the brainstorming technique, greater utility can be achieved and more directed ideas will emerge. The following process describes this modification.

- Prepare *what* and *how* a brainstorming session will be conducted.

- Follow one or more of the methods and techniques to generate ideas. The ideas stimulation process will be more fun than just *let's go around the table and generate ideas.*
- Never completely discard an idea. Keep a record for future sessions if the idea must be discarded for the session where it was generated.

The basic steps for brainstorming are:

1. **Warm-up**—Provide session participants with an exercise to enable them to clear their mind and be ready to participate in the session.

2. **Record**—It is recommended that a person be acquired outside of the team since team member attention should be directed to the task at hand and not diluted with the duties of a recorder. This person records the ideas on large sheets of paper located in the front of the room. Variations could be the use of a computer and projector system with the scribe recording an idea electronically and simultaneously projecting it for participants to see. Instead of a normal mouse, a stylus could be used to enable immediate drawing for connection of thoughts and illustrations. An electronic large whiteboard is another possibility. This device enables a printout of what has been written on the board. The more traditional chalk and board approach in conjunction with a digital camera could be used to provide a record of what is written on the board.

3. **Present/Clarify the Problem Statement/Session Objective**—Define a Problem Statement/Session Objective before the session. Present it to the team with a minimum of explanation. Give the team time to discuss and understand it.

4. **Generate ideas**—The session facilitator asks for ideas. There doesn't have to be any particular order as to who speaks up. The task is to generate many ideas. Everyone should participate. The facilitator should keep the session fun but on track. The facilitator is obtained from outside the team and assigned the job as facilitator for the duration of the project.

A worksheet for a brainstorming session is provided in Appendix D.3 and an example of a completed worksheet in Appendix D.4.

Force Field Analysis

The Force Field Analysis is a very useful creative problem-solving technique. It was developed by Kurt Lewin in 1947. It is valued because it focuses on forces already working in a problem or situation (Lewin 1951).

At the beginning, a detailed analysis is conducted of the problem or situation. From the analysis, the forces *driving* the problem or situation are identified as well as forces *inhibiting* improvement. Once all these forces are identified, creative ideas can be generated to alter or eliminate these forces and/or introduce new forces in order to achieve the required improvement.

Pros

A Force Field Analysis:

- Identifies the forces driving the problem or situation and inhibiting improvement.
- Allows everyone to participate.
- Enables flexibility since a wide range of idea-generating techniques are needed for stimulation.
- Requires that all team members participate and do their assign tasks.

Cons

A Force Field Analysis:

- Team members must be familiar with the problem or situation in order to identify the driving and inhibiting forces.
- Familiarity could result in contributing forces not being identified.
- Requires detail work on the part of team members.
- Detail work must be completed on schedule and as defined.

The basic steps for the Force Field Analysis are:

1. **Define the problem or situation.** It is critical that a clear problem or situation statement be defined and understood

by all team members. Once established, the statement should be posted for the team to see. Also, it should be printed on handout sheets and given to team members for reference.

2. **Fine-tune the problem or situation statement.** Look at the current problem or situation and ask questions such as:

   - Why does the problem or situation exist?
   - What changes have occurred?

   Use brainstorming to list everything about the current problem/situation to establish the *what is*. Then ask questions to determine *what should be*.

   - What should be going on?
   - How would the forces be distributed?

3. **List all the forces *driving* the problem or situation.** Make a complete list. Don't leave out forces considered too small or insignificant. Challenge the list with *what's missing?*

4. **List all the forces that *inhibit* improvement.** Make a complete list. Don't leave out forces considered too small or insignificant. Challenge the list with the *what's missing?*

5. **Review all the forces.** The team should now determine the significant driving and inhibiting forces.

6. **Determine impact of forces on the Problem/Situation Statement.** The significant driving and inhibiting forces from step 5 are now used to determine whether or not changes should be made to the problem/situation statement. For example: "Late deliveries are not acceptable" changed to "Vulcan transmissions must be delivered to the customer within two hours."

7. **Start creative idea generation.** The team can use any creative idea-generating technique. The team makes the choice.

8. **Evaluate the ideas.** The team evaluates the ideas relative to the problem/situation statement. The outcome of candidate ideas then becomes input for the innovative process.

A facilitator from outside the team should be used for the force field analysis session. Depending on the competency of the individual, the same facilitator used for the brainstorming session could be used for the force field session.

Forms to support the force field analysis are contained in Appendix D.5. Also, an example is shown in Appendix D.6.

TRIZ

TRIZ is a Russian acronym, which when translated means: *Theory of the Solution of Inventive-Type Problems.* An *inventive-type* problem is one that contains, within the problem, one or more technical conflicts. Genrich Altshuller developed the TRIZ method in 1946(Altshuller 1998). The method is practiced worldwide. It was introduced in the United States in 1991 where it continues to be developed(Kowalick 1999).

TRIZ research began with the hypothesis that there are universal principles of invention that form the basis to advance technology. Identifying and coding these principles would enable the process of invention to be more predictable. People could be taught the process. Over 1.5 million patents have been examined with about 500,000 considered the most inventive. Findings indicated that 1. problems and solutions were repeated across industries and sciences; 2. patterns of technical evolution were repeated across industries and sciences, and 3. creative solutions used scientific effects outside the field where they were developed.

Products, services, processes, and systems can be created and improved with the TRIZ method. TRIZ provokes the creative and innovative processes by technical contradiction. A technical contradiction occurs when a person or team is working to improve one characteristic, or parameter, of a technical system and causes another characteristic or parameter of the system to deteriorate. A compromise solution is then reached. With TRIZ, no compromises are required. The ideal solution can be reached without having a compromise, or without having to trade-off one product feature for another.

Technical system parameters could involve for example: weight, volume, speed, flexibility, size, and color. These parameters describe the physical state of the technical system.

One of the tools used to overcome technical contradictions is called *Principles.* But this is just one of the tools. In fact, there are several tools that are highly effective. An illustration that is quite popular for the use of technical conflicts—and for how they can be resolved using Inventive Principles—is the process of shaving. The *shaving system* parameter most likely to be changed to give customers a close shave, is the sharpness of the edge of the razor blade. However, when the edge of the razor blade is made very, very sharp in order to create a closer shave for the shaver, this also makes it easier to cut the skin. The skin is cut and blood flows. In this instance, there is both an improving feature—the razor blade is sharpened to improve closeness of the shave—and a worsening feature—sharpening the razor blade makes the skin easier to cut, resulting in nicks and cuts. This is an example of a technical conflict.

So what can be done to solve the technical conflicts, and in particular, this problem with the razor blade? One approach suggested is to apply TRIZ Inventive Principles to the problem. For example, TRIZ suggests the use of the principle of *multiplicity:* multiply the objects involved. One of the major objects involved is the razor blade itself. *Multiplying* it means two or more razor blades; this leads to such products as multiple blade razors, and blade cartridges that are very successful in the market place.

Another example involves the *Periodic Action Principle.* This Principle states that one continuous action should be replaced with a periodic, or pulsating action. Example: Can water be used to cut steel? When a continuous stream of water is directed on a $\frac{1}{2}$ inch thick steel plate no cutting action occurs. However, pulse the stream of water at a very high pressure and the water cuts the steel without any difficulty.

Other TRIZ tools include a prediction-type tool that predicts the steps of evolution that lead to significant increases in product or process-performance indicators. Usually it takes years or even decades for such evolution to occur, but with TRIZ, system evolution can occur almost overnight or in days, weeks, and months, depending on the product or process.

Large and small companies are beginning to use the TRIZ method. Like most new methods, the people using TRIZ represent the forward thinkers in their companies. Before embarking on using the TRIZ method, team members need to be trained. This usually takes 3 to 5 days. TRIZ software programs are used to support the explorations of the team. TRIZ software is available from the Renaissance Leadership Institute. This software is very user friendly and reduces the time for solutions.

These are the general Pros and Cons for TRIZ.

Pros for TRIZ:

- Straightforward technique easily applied after training to simple- and medium-level complex problems.
- Produces breakthrough results.

Cons for TRIZ:

- Requires several days of training.
- Highly complex problems require TRIZ expert facilitator.

TRIZ Resources

The TRIZ journal provides articles and timely insights on the use of TRIZ methods as experienced by practitioners worldwide. The journal can be found on the Internet at: http://www.triz-journal.com.

The TRIZ University is found on the Internet at: http://www.trizuniversity.com

The California Institute of Technology listing for "Creating Breakthrough Products" can be found on the Internet at: http://www.irc.caltech.edu. This is a TRIZ course offering. Usually, it is offered twice annually.

TRIZ Books and software can be found through Breakthrough Press on the Internet at: http://www.bythewaybooks.com.

TRIZ expertise, software, books, and advancing TRIZ state-of-the-art is found at the Renaissance Leadership Institute, Inc. P.O. Box 659, 9907 Camper Lane, Oregon House, CA 95962. Telephone: (916) 692–1944.

Mind Mapping

If you like diagrams, you'll find mind mapping is a lot of fun and at the same time, a great tool to generate creative ideas. In the early 1970s, Tony Buzan discovered that using a diagram technique of jotting down ideas helped to spark additional creative ideas. Mind mapping works on the principle that the mind operates best when ideas are allowed to flow freely (Buzan 1983). Mind mapping enables the free flow of ideas while systematically recording them. In so doing, a diagram is created for team members to see and this visual feedback stimulates other ideas.

Pros of mind mapping:

- Generate a lot of creative ideas with a diagram for visual feedback stimulation.
- Everyone can participate.
- Generates a quantity of creative ideas in a short time.
- Uses the whole brain.

Cons of mind mapping:

- Only produces ideas.
- Participants may jump into idea generation without preparation.
- Participants not shown how to get the novel ideas. This show of brilliance is just supposed to occur.

The basic steps for mind mapping are:

1. **Define the topic**—Write the name or description of the topic (e.g. problem/situation, idea/concept) in the center of a large piece of paper and draw a circle around it.
2. **Identify major elements**—Use the brainstorming technique to identify major elements that relate to the problem/situation. Each element is represented by a line that is drawn from the problem/situation circle. Continue to brainstorm major elements until the team is satisfied that major elements are identified. These main branches can be in separate color from the problem/situation circle.
3. **Identify support branches**—Use brainstorming to identify branches that support each major element line. In this process, sub-branches can be identified. At the discretion of the team, step 3 could be combined with step 2. In other words, when a major element is identified, the branches and sub-branches can be identified at the same time. Branches can be drawn with a different color than the

major element line. Sub-branches can be drawn in a different color than the branches and major element lines.

4. **Group Ideas**—Ideas shown on the mind map can be grouped into common categories or themes and evaluated to identify candidate ideas for input to the innovative process.

An outside facilitator should be used for mind mapping. A blank mind mapping worksheet is contained in Appendix D.7. An example of mind mapping is shown in Appendix D.8.

Free Association

Association is defined in the dictionary as the process of forming mental connections or bonds between sensations, ideas or memories. It works through three primary laws originally taught by the ancient Greeks: contiguity, similarity and contrast (Higgins 1994).

According to the dictionary,

- Contiguity means nearness—for example: when you see a beach, you think of swimming.
- Similarity means that one object or thought will remind you of a similar object or thought—for example: when you see a dollar bill your think about a million dollars.
- Contrast refers to dissimilarities that are nearly opposites— profit/loss, pure/defective, on-time/late, rise/fall.

Free Association draws on whatever comes into your mind using a word or picture to stimulate thinking. It is a process of making mental connections between two different thoughts. The purpose is to trigger new thoughts about a problem/situation. These thoughts will lead to creative ideas as potential solutions to the problem/situation.

Pros of free association:

- Generates thoughts that lead to creative ideas.
- Excellent for setting direction.
- Removes thinking inhibitors.
- Stimulates chains of thoughts for creative ideas.
- Demonstrates the power of linking thoughts to create ideas.

Cons of free association:

- Requires patience that thoughts will lead to creative ideas as solutions.
- Participants need to be free thinking and allow the technique to work.
- Looking for thoughts initially rather than solutions.

The basic steps for Free Association are:

1. List numbers from 1 to 20. Allow a space to write next to each number. A blank form is shown in Appendix D.9 and example in Appendix D.10.
2. On line 1, put one word that defines the problem/situation.
3. Look at the word on line 1 and write down the one word thought on line 2 that comes to mind when thinking about the word on line 1.
4. Look at the word on line 2 and write down the one-word thought that comes to mind on line 3 when thinking about the word on line 2.
5. Repeat the process for lines 3 through 20.
6. Look at the ten words for insight to the problem/situation
7. Use the words that stand out and brainstorm with these words to generate ideas.
8. Output from the brainstorming may provide thought for new associations. This process is continued until creative ideas are identified as suitable candidates for the innovative process.

A Free Association flow chart is shown in Figure 5.5.

WEB SITES FOR CREATIVITY

The reader is encouraged to take advantage of the many search engines on the Internet. Here are a few: http://www.altavista.com, http://www.metacrawler.com, http://www.yahoo.com

A number of words and phrases can be used depending on the topic of interest to be searched. For example: team creativity, creative process, idea creation, creativity awards, customer-supplier creativity, supplier creative process, brainstorming, force field analysis, mind mapping, and inventions.

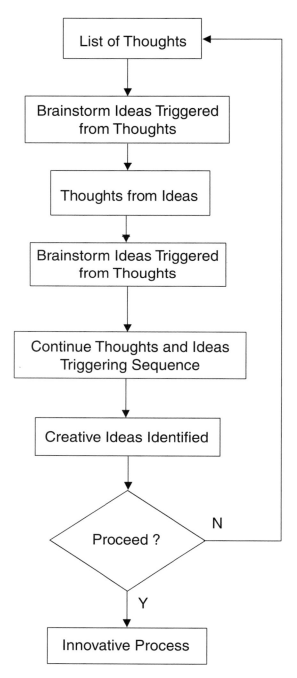

Figure 5.5.   Free association process flow chart.

These are but a few of the web sites dedicated to creativity. Have fun surfing!

http://www.DirectedCreativity.com. Provides descriptions of creative models and tools along with other resources such as random word lists, application examples, and downloadable articles.

http://www.triz-journal.com. The premier site for the latest thinking on TRIZ and its applications.

http://www.creativesparks.org. The National Center for Creativity, Inc. is a non-profit organization that organizes and manages seminars that provide techniques and concepts that help in creativity and innovative thinking in various business and civic settings.

http://www.ozemail.com.au/~caveman/Creative/ A great web site referred to as *Charles Cave* in Sidney, Australia. It contains outstanding resource listings on books, software, creative information, and links to other web sites on creativity.

CREATIVITY TRAINING FOR TEAM MEMBERS

Knowledge to understand any endeavor is essential for success. Team members are given education and training on the creative process and how this attitude and behavior can influence the outcome. All education and training is done with all team members present. If for some reason the full team is not present for an education and training session, then the session is rescheduled. The principle is *learn together and work together.*

There are six key factors, Figure 5.6, that need to be satisfied before the team starts the education and training process

Willingness to learn—Each team member must be willing to learn the principles that form the basis for creativity. In so doing, a team member not only learns, but also helps to set a positive learning environment for other team members.

Competency to understand the material—In reality, the principles for the creative process are simple and straightforward. Since team members are selected, this

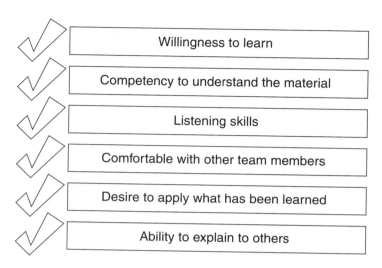

Figure 5.6.   Preparation factors.

factor should always be satisfied. There could be an unusual situation when this isn't true.

Listening skill—Each team member is given a test to determine the extent of their listening ability. As needed, team members are trained to demonstrate a level of listening proficiency.

Comfortable with other team members—Each team member must feel comfortable in terms of intellectual exchanges.

Desire to apply what has been learned—This represents a *can do spirit* and excitement in discovering new knowledge and being able to put the new knowledge to work.

Ability to explain to others—Each team member must be able to clearly explain his or her ideas covering both pros and cons. He or she must be willing to respond to criticism in a non-confrontational manner.

Figure 5.7 shows five fundamental courses that team members are taught to support their involvement with the creativity process.

Creativity Preparation Courses

1. Thinking while in the midst of chaos

2. Non-constrained thinking

3. Being independent, yet a team participant

4. Letting go of idea ownership

5. Consensus process

Figure 5.7. Creativity preparation courses.

1. Thinking in the midst of chaos. This is the skill to think under pressure while having numerous distractions.
2. Non-constrained thinking. This idea is similar to a Zen *no-mind* in that all things are possible and should be considered.
3. Being independent, yet a team member. This apparent contradiction says that a person does not loose individual identity while being accountable as a team member.
4. Letting go of idea ownership. This involves being part of the collective *brain trust* and not being pulled down by ego.
5. Consensus process. Participate in the consensus process and support the consensus position of the team.

CREATIVITY TRAINING WHEN NEW MEMBERS ARE ADDED

New and existing members are exposed to the same training. This serves as a refresher for the existing members. The guiding principle is simple: the team does everything together when it comes to creativity. Training isn't an exception.

PROBLEM/SITUATION STATEMENT

The team receives the problem/situation statement from the team sponsors. This is an agreed to statement on the part of the sponsors. Background about the problem/situation is provided.

The team evaluates the problem/situation statement to establish the validity. All too often a problem/situation statement may not be correct in terms of providing a solution to the right problem/situation.

The process steps to validate the problem/situation statement are as follows:

- Why does the problem/situation exist? (Asked until a root cause(s) is stated).
- What is the cause(s) for the problem/situation?
- When is a solution required?
- What are the consequences of not having a solution?
- Clear statement of the criteria that a solution must satisfy.
- Agreement by the sponsors and team.
- The idea-generation process can be started.

A worksheet for this process is provided in Appendix D.11.

CREATIVITY USED IN A TEAM SETTING

We were working on a problem and things just clicked. I felt as though I could read the other person's mind. And the other person had the same feeling. Some people call this *chemistry,* Figure 5.8. An essential ingredient for the creative process is to work with two or more people. Its foundation is built on high curiosity and the maturity to not *attack* the other person's thoughts especially in the developmental stage that leads to an idea. Listening plays a key role since being a good listener strengthens the confidence in the person doing the talking. In so doing, the flow of thoughts can develop fast and not be choked off by criticism.

The team needs practice in following the rules for creativity in a team setting. This begins with each team member understanding the rules. These rules aren't intended to stifle the creative process, quite the contrary, they are intend to create a nur-

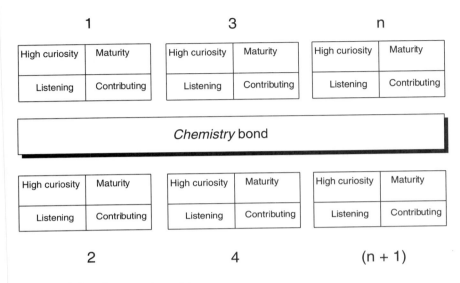

Figure 5.8. Team chemistry.

turing environment for creativity to thrive. If a timetable is established to produce creative ideas by the end of the second week or whatever time schedule, this could take the fun out of being creative. Co-leaders keep the schedule fun, yet don't lose sight of required output.

To be mentally creative, a person must let his or her guard down. He or she must explore unconstrained mental boundaries without any inhibitions or intimidation. Once each individual understands these basic tenants, the creative process is positioned for start-up.

Creativity in a team setting must avoid the *it's my idea* notion. For creativity to be successful, each team member has to surrender ownership on an individual basis and take ownership for the *whole* of the team's creativity. This can be very exciting and exhilarating when the team is generating ideas.

The team needs to agree that the problem they are seeking to solve must be agreed to by all the members. Further, each member must be able to describe the problem and the current impact the problem is causing. Unless understanding and true belief in the problem exist, the creative process will be hampered simply because the mental energy to be creative will be contaminated by doubt and perhaps confusion about the problem description. As an example, a team is working to provide a creative solution for a bioengineered corn plant that resists all current pests. If one or more team member has a value system that you shouldn't fool around with Mother Nature, then he or she certainly will be mentally constrained to come up with creative solutions. How can this situation be detected? It takes honesty on the part of each team member to disclose that he or she has a personal problem or philosophical difference with the assignment.

TEAM CREATIVE MOOD EXERCISES

As stated previously, clearing the mind and focusing are essential steps to generating creative ideas. The team needs to move into a proper mental state to achieve these steps. Conditioning exercises are recommended.

Clear the Mind—Sensory deprivation or contradictions provide ways to help clear the mind. A listing is provided as follows:

- Stand on your head for one minute.
- Create a contradiction such as putting a T-shirt on backwards.
- Write your name upside down at least 20 times.
- Darken the lights in the room and close your eyes for 10 minutes.
- Be silent for 10 minutes.
- Listen to the sounds of whales.
- Touch a stone or glass marble.
- Look into a mirror.

Focus—Increase consciousness by practicing to eliminate a common word in what you say. The idea is to create a situation where you stop and think before you speak. As an example: eliminate the word *the* from what you say. Become oblivious to activity around you. Seek the flow of focus much like athletes achieve. In Zen, it is becoming one with the thought or object. It is recommended that you practice your focus technique before, during, and after the session. Being able to focus is a skill, and it can be learned.

Also, on a daily basis the team needs to do the following:

- Keep the problem/situation in perspective.
- Keep a *we will succeed* attitude.
- Stay focused. Recognize when focus is lost and make an adjustment.
- Balance tension with humor.
- Engage in many conversations. Thinking for long periods of time without conversation degrades the creative thinking process.

TEAM DIVERSITY

Diversity of viewpoint is essential for the team to produce creative ideas as proposed solutions. There must exist a common chemistry and the bonding of team members for maximum effectiveness of the team.

The diagram, Figure 5.9, illustrates that members operate off a common chemistry bus. This does not suggest that members are clones. It illustrates that common dimensions are needed for the chemistry to exist and bonding to occur. Certainly members possess other dimensions that define their individuality. Each team member is unique.

Diversity means different views for a given situation. The expression of these different viewpoints must be done in the spirit of sharing and advancing ideas. If they become a destructive element for argument, they will curtail the creative flow process.

WORK ENVIRONMENT FOR TEAM CREATIVITY

The best work environment is decided by the team. Yes, the team could rent a house on the beach to do their work. The only provision, the work must get done.

Obviously, the team must be comfortable not only with the physical environment, but also the influence of other people working in this environment. Basic principles of what has been

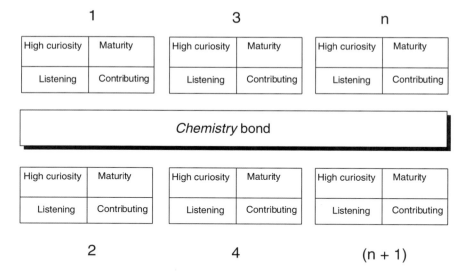

Figure 5.9. Common bus.

learned for creative environments need to be followed but should not dictate totally the team environment.

The use of databases and computers and other equipment must be readily accessible to team members. Team members are encouraged to simulate the problem/issue situation to have not only a constant reminder in their environment, but also a visual representation in the form of a model or statement. This environmental reinforcement contributes to the mental picture carried in the mind of each team member and provides consistent visual input.

Depending on the complexity and seriousness of the required problem/issue, team members should be afforded all the necessary resources in their environment. The environment should promote learning. The need for free exchange of ideas among team members must exist during formal and informal sessions. In fact, a mantra when discussing an idea should be . . . "from your idea I learned and see that" . . . This mantra offers a complementary and positive method in building a idea staircase, Figure 5.10. When climbing the idea staircase, the intention is to continue to build and reinforce the original idea. In this process, breakthrough thinking is ignited from the rapid crescendo of idea climbing.

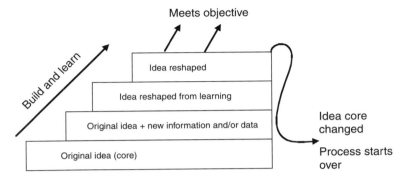

Meets objective

Build and learn

Idea reshaped

Idea reshaped from learning

Original idea + new information and/or data

Original idea (core)

Idea core changed

Process starts over

Figure 5.10. Idea learning staircase.

The work environment can be assessed for creativity. The KEYS instrument is used for this purpose (Amabile 1996). Also, information about this instrument is found at internet web site: http//:www.ccl.org/products/keys/keysdetail.htm.

INNOVATION FOCUS AND CREATIVITY

The Innovation Focus (IF) instrument is covered in chapter 4. The IF helps an individual determine their preference for involvement with innovation. When a person has an innovation focus, what is their corresponding creative component? Is it possible that a person with a strong IF would not be as creative as required to participate on the team?

To be a successful innovator, the person needs to understand the creative process and possess creative thinking skills and be motivated to generate creative ideas. With an appreciation of creativity, an innovative person may not overlook an excellent creative idea because the outcome of the solution for the creative idea isn't easily translated as an acceptable implementation.

One tends to classify creative people as dreamers and innovative people as doers. To a large extent when people are left to their own boundaries and standards, this is a true statement. However, when involved in a process, people tend to do equally well in a customer-supplier innovation team setting as both creator and innovator.

BENCHMARKING FOR CREATIVE IDEAS

Benchmarking for creative ideas can be a part of the creative idea generation process. However, it is not a central part of the process. Learning how either the same or similar problems or situations are solved by others can provide meaningful input. The caution is not to allow the team to stop with this insight and simply adapt the solution from benchmarking. If benchmarking is used, it should be done after considerable energy on the part of the team has been expended to create ideas. In other words, benchmarking is not the *cure all* for the problem or situation.

Benchmarking when used properly should stimulate the generation of creative ideas rather than curtail or limit idea generation. By just adapting what has been benchmarked may not necessarily provide a solution that enables the adapter to gain a substantial lead over the competition. This is especially the case if the benchmarked item (for example, product, service, process, system) represents what the competition is already doing yet is new and innovative to the adapter.

CREATIVITY ON DEMAND

In terms of the pure creative world of an artist, the only time constraint may be that imposed by the artist. In the business world, time is money. Solutions to problems or issues are mandatory within a given time frame. This becomes very true in emergency and threatening situations, for example, space travel, oil or gas wells burning out of control.

The Apollo 13 leaking fuel situation is an excellent example of customer and supplier working together to resolve a very serious problem threatening the safe return of the spacecraft (NASA 1970). Time was of the essence.

> "Houston, we've got a problem." This declaration on the part of astronaut Jack Swigert launched the creative energy on the part of the mission control customer and supplier team. At 55 hours and 46 minutes into the Apollo 13 mission everything was working according to plan. Nine minutes later, oxygen tank No. 2 blew up, causing No. 1 tank to also fail. The Apollo 13 command module's

normal supply of electricity, light and water was lost and they were 200,000 miles from Earth. Very serious problems indeed. Both the astronauts and Mission Control got the idea that the only place to get fuel was from the Lunar Module.

Ground controllers in Houston faced a formidable task. Completely new procedures had to be written and tested in the simulator before being passed up to the crew. The navigation problem had to be solved: essentially how, when, and in what attitude to burn the Lunar Module descent engine to provide a safe return to Earth.

A most remarkable achievement of Mission Control was quickly developing procedures for powering up the Command Module after cold days of inactivity. Flight controllers wrote the documents for this creative and innovative solution in three days, instead of the usual three months.

Removal of carbon dioxide was also a concern. There were enough lithium hydroxide canisters, which remove carbon dioxide from the spacecraft, but the square canisters from Command Module were not compatible with the round openings in the Lunar Module environment system. There were four cartridges from the Lunar Module and four from the backpacks, counting backups. However, the Lunar Module was designed to support two men for two days and now was being asked to care for three men for nearly four days. After a day and a half in the Lunar Module, a warning light showed that the carbon dioxide had built up to a dangerous level. Mission Control devised a way to attach the Command Module canisters to the Lunar Module system by using plastic bags, cardboard, and tape—all materials carried on board.

Mission Control figured out how to align the Command Module's navigational problem by using the Lunar Module navigation system and aligning the navigational system with the sun as a star rather than a real star since damage to the Lunar Module made it impossible to sight real stars. This was accomplished by astronaut Jim Lovell working with Mission Control. (NASA 1970)

Yes, the creative-innovative processes work under serious time pressure. Just recall the Apollo 13 mission when inspiration is needed.

Experience with customer-supplier innovation teams over several decades suggests that time pressure isn't always a negative factor in causing intense focus to produce an abundance of very good creative ideas.

To a large extent this emphasizes that behind creative thinking there are five time proven principles. These are: 1. Clear the Mind, 2. Focus, 3. Seek Patterns, 4. Adjust, and 5. Select. In an intense situation, the mind tends to clear itself. If panic occurs, this can be very disruptive to the creative process since a clear mind and focus are nonexistent.

HIGH OUTPUT TEAM CREATIVITY

Time compression caused by an emergency is the best clearing of the air for high output creativity. Members must be mentally focused to have a survival view. The sole purpose for existing is related directly to producing creative ideas that are acceptable and plausible. This intense and extreme mental adaptation sets the stage for high output creativity.

The situation can be simulated by provoking creativity with the use of catalysts such as pictures, words, and objects. However, in so doing the participants must understand the process before they participate, otherwise, the effectiveness will not be as great.

What are the absolute foolproof methods to achieve a *clear the air* mental process for high output creativity? Each member must develop his or her own stimulation for mental conditioning to clear their mind and enter into an extreme focus. This isn't a mental trance but could be described as a mental state where disruptive elements do not influence concentration. It would be similar to a concert pianist absorbed in playing a difficult music piece.

Clear the air really addresses the point that each member clears his or her own air. They must place themselves in a full alert mental state. This better ensures that the *white moment* of creative discovery (the Ah-Ha, the light bulb turning on) will occur.

Table 5.2. Creative progress.

	Idea	Idea	Physical	Process Speed	Idea
Measure	Value	Quantity	Weight	Cycle time	Acceptance
Metric Measurement	Scale 8 (1 to 10)	Number 20	Pounds 50	Hours 10	Number 5

CREATIVE PROGRESS

What gets attention, gets done. The need for establishing measures, metrics, and measurements provides evidence on how well the team is doing. This status is important for all concerned.

Creating ideas for the sake of creating ideas at some point in time must be aligned with the reality that the output of creative ideas suitable for the innovative process are required. Progress must be defined and reported to the sponsors.

For definition purposes and to better ensure a common understanding of terms, the following is offered:

- What is a measure? A property of a person, place, or thing used for comparison.
- What is a metric? A basic unit that can be used to give value to a measure.
- What is a measurement? A data point quantifying a measure in terms of a specific metric.

Examples of a measure, metric, and measurement are shown in Table 5.2.

CREATIVE IDEAS EVALUATION

The team generated abundant creative ideas as potential solutions for the problem/situation statement. These ideas are now evaluated. Ideas that offer merit as potential solutions are transferred to the innovative process.

The evaluation of creative ideas uses a straightforward matrix approach as shown in Table 5.3. The *value* of an idea is associated with rows. It is classified as low, medium, and high.

Table 5.3. Creative idea evaluation—primary.

The *simplicity* of an idea is associated with columns. It is classified as low, medium, and high.

Value applies to a process, product, service, or system depending on the idea and ability of the idea to satisfy the problem/situation statement. It has the same application as simplicity. The level of value contribution is rated as low, medium, or high.

Simplicity applies to a process, product, service, or system depending on the idea and the problem/situation statement. It has the same application as value. The level of simplicity contribution is rated as low, medium, or high.

Team members consider each creative idea and rate the idea according to low, medium, or high value. Team agreement is based on consensus. Next, team members consider each creative idea and rate the idea according to low, medium, or high simplicity. Team agreement is based on consensus.

Creative ideas that are placed in the *high value* and *high simplicity* cell are selected as first choice for transfer to the innovative process.

Table 5.4. Creative idea evaluation—secondary.

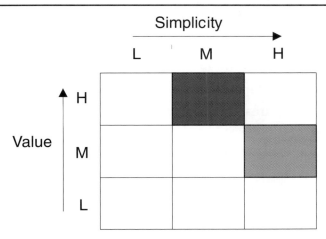

Secondary level creative ideas are located in cells of *high value* and *medium simplicity* and *medium value* and *high simplicity*. This is illustrated in Table 5.4. These ideas are transferred to the innovative process as back-up to the primary.

LESSONS LEARNED

1. Agree on the problem/situation statement.

2. Agree on the criteria for accepting a creative solution.

3. Set a schedule.

4. Define measures, metrics, and take measurements to determine progress.

5. Encourage informal discussion.

6. Keep comments/dialogue constructive but realistic when appropriate to do so. Don't say an idea is worthless. Rather, "We can learn from this idea, thanks for sharing."

7. Keep a sense of humor throughout the creative process.

8. Avoid getting involved with a creative idea generating technique to the exclusion as to why the technique is being used in the first place.

9. Avoid mental and physical fatigue.

SUMMARY

1. Everyone can be creative within his or her field. It is a learned skill.

2. Creativity is defined as the generation of ideas. Innovations are the implementation of ideas. Though creativity and innovation are treated separately, in reality the two processes create a *solution system*. The processes are dependent on each other.

3. The creative process is a fluid process. It conforms to no particular set of steps. Depending on the problem or situation, the creative process should satisfy these conditions:
   - Reason for the creativity—problem, issue, improvement.
   - Techniques to be used.
   - Idea evolution/building.
   - Evaluation of the ideas generated.
   - Accepted ideas as input to the innovative process.

4. Team members must prepare to participate in the creative process. Critical activities involve relaxing, clearing the mind, and being able to focus on the problem or situation to generate ideas and see linkages with ideas to evolve to higher level ideas as candidates for the innovative process.

5. A model, Figure 5.4, illustrates the steps for idea generation. A facilitator for the idea generation process is chosen by the team. Record keeping is essential for the creative process. A person other than a team member should keep the records. This could be included in the duties for the facilitator. This frees team members to concentrate on the creative process.

6. Common techniques used for the creative process are brainstorming, force analysis, TRIZ, mind-mapping, and free association. There are hundreds of techniques that teams can choose. It is suggested that the team choose those techniques that the team can use easily to produce results

such as generating ideas and providing accepted ideas for the innovative process.

7. Before team members charge off to display their creative talents, the team should be given baseline creativity training.

8. The problem or situation statement represents the *forcing function* for the creative process. It is the reason for the team to engage in the creative process. It is essential that the problem or situation statement be understood by the team members and, as necessary, challenged and changed to represent the *real* problem or situation statement.

9. Creativity in a team setting works best when a chemistry bond exists for team members. In essence, the chemistry enables team members to be free of criticism in an environment that is filled with high curiosity and the excitement of discovery that fuels further involvement. The common elements for chemistry are not intended to have team members that are cloned. Quite the contrary, team members retain their individuality but are able to function with a common chemistry.

10. Benchmarking for creative ideas relative to the problem or situation should be left as a last step in the creative process. Benchmarking when used properly should stimulate the generation of creative ideas rather than curtail or limit idea generation.

11. Creativity can be accomplished in a time compressed situation. The Apollo 13 leaking fuel situation is an excellent example.

12. Creative progress needs to be established to ensure requirements of the sponsors are met. Measures, metrics, and measurements provide the evidence on how well the team is doing.

13. Creative ideas need to be evaluated to identify ideas that offer merit as potential solutions for transfer to the innovative process. An evaluation matrix approach is

covered in Table 5.3 for primary consideration and Table 5.4 for secondary.

14. Web sites for creativity are covered. Surfing these sites will lead to other site discoveries.

15. Lessons learned regarding the creative process applied to the customer-supplier innovation team are covered.

16. The reader is presented with a series of questions regarding the creative process applied to the customer-supplier innovation team.

QUESTIONS

1. What is creativity?

2. How is creativity used in a team setting?

3. What are examples of team creativity?

4. What training should the team members be given in creativity?

5. What is the process for creativity training when new members are added to the team?

6. What are the creative techniques?

7. How is the transition made from idea generation to implementing the best idea?

8. What process is used to determine the best idea?

9. How are ideas generated?

10. How is the problem/issue defined that forms the focus for idea generation?

11. What work environment is best suited for creativity?

12. What are web sites for creativity?

13. What is TRIZ? How can TRIZ be used?

14. What are the results obtained with TRIZ?

15. How do world class customer-suppliers use the creative process?

16. Can anyone be creative? What do the experts say?

17. What is done in a team situation so as not to stifle creativity of each of the team members?

18. What type of exercise can the member and the team do to move themselves into a creative mode?

19. What are lessons learned from using creativity in a team setting?

20. Can the creative process be time compressed?

21. Is it necessary to time compress the creative process?

22. How can the creative process be time compressed?

23. Can the creative process be treated as a stand-alone process or should it be coupled with innovation?

24. If the creative process is treated as a system, does this in itself stifle the generation of ideas?

25. What happens when the team or some other source requires a schedule for creative output?

26. What type of *clear the air* experience is used for high output creativity?

27. If people have an innovation focus, what's their creative component? Could a person with a strong innovative focus not be as creative as required?

28. What's the role of diversity in the team and the value contributed to creating ideas?

29. Should the team benchmark for creative ideas? When should benchmarking be done?

30. Is the creative process just about producing ideas? Or is it focusing on best solutions to the stated problem?

31. How is the creative process for the customer-supplier innovation team defined?

32. What is the daily routine for the team to exercise the creative process?

33. What measures, metrics, and measurements are used to determine progress?

Innovation for Payoff

"Wealth is created by the capitalization of innovation—by linking new discoveries to customers' wants and needs."

Lester Thurow, Economist

WHAT IS INNOVATION?

Innovation requires the act to use a newly created idea. As covered in chapter 5, many ideas are created but few actually are used as solutions. Innovation brings the aspect of risk taking to the level of investing in the newly created idea to make its use successful. The intent of the innovation is to provide a solution that impacts the profitability of the customer-supplier. The incentive to use innovation as a competitive lever is being adapted by large and small companies alike. After all, with the global economy and the access to materials, equipment, and technology that levels the playing field, the one factor that provides a huge advantage is innovation of products, services, processes, and systems. Given competitive pricing and equal quality, the end-user will be attracted to the innovation that the product offers. An example of this would be, a rental car that includes a Ground Positioning System at no extra cost for the driver to use real-time map locating as a navigational aid. Another example would be a product that can be diagnosed remotely for identification of a pending or existing problem and then provides the corrective solution with the user doing nothing but making the hook-up with an on-line diagnostic center. This is exactly what companies like Dell Computer and Microsoft do to support end-users of their products.

In the early 1980s continuous improvement via Kaizen was heralded as the approach to become competitive. Many American companies adopted the Japanese's Kaizen approach(Imai 1986). With this approach, companies made progress. However, people became generally conditioned to subtle improvements with results that were not always immediately visible. When introduced in the mid 1980s, Kaizen with its methodical, incremental, and slower approach to continuous improvement was appropriate for the American business environment. American companies were discovering the value and competitive advantage of quality. However, times have changed. Global competition is aggressive. Technologies are rapidly changing. Now, quality is considered a given in the global market. "Incrementalism is innovation's worst enemy" (Peters 1997). Innovation represents the best sustaining competitive advantage. And, there isn't any reason why innovation cannot be exercised on a continuous basis once the process is institutionalized in companies. Visionary companies such as General Electric, 3M, Corning Inc., and John Deere have and continue to use innovation as a competitive advantage. L.D. Desimone, Chairman and CEO of 3M has said "to sustain growth, we need innovation. To sustain innovation, we need the best people. To sustain our people, we need to constantly challenge them . . . with the best practices, processes and ideas to help serve our customers." (Special Advertising 1997). The Kellogg Company's Board, facing declining earnings, appointed a new CEO, Carlos Guiterrez. In outlining his approach for a turn-around, he declared "we have to drive earnings through innovation" (Taylor III 1999).

Innovation can bring great advances in changes to products, services, processes, and systems. These advances cannot be just a *one-shot* phenomenon. In fact, customer-supplier innovation teams must engage in continuous innovation in order to lead the competition and to meet user demands.

TEAM WEARS TWO HATS

The customer-supplier innovation team wears two hats. One as creator and evaluator of ideas and the other to find and implement solutions.

The innovative process involves the following:

- Evaluate proposed primary and secondary creative ideas in terms of satisfying the *use* criteria. The use criteria is defined before the team begins their project. This criteria may be updated as greater understanding of the intended use evolves. Generally, it involves a problem/situation statement.
- There may be a situation where team members improve on primary and secondary creative ideas.
- A simulation of the creative ideas may be made and/or a physical prototype built and tested.
- Findings from the simulation and/or prototype will be used to determine the risk of introducing an idea as the solution.
- The team will make a presentation to the sponsors.
- The team will be responsible for implementing the approved idea solution. This involves monitoring the effectiveness of the idea solution.

The innovative process is illustrated with Figure 6.1 flow chart. The differences between the creative and innovative process is highlighted in Table 6.1.

INNOVATIVE WORK ENVIRONMENT

Like the creative work environment, the innovative work environment must be able to support the customer-supplier innovation team with resources and the encouragement to operate and produce the expected result for the project.

In the best situation, the team defines their physical work environment. In some cases this may not be possible, but in all cases the physical comfort of the team is primary. The intention is to define the work environment such that it becomes transparent in the mind and view of the team as they become engrossed in the innovative task at hand.

As with the creative process, a proper environment must exist for the customer-supplier innovation team to achieve breakthrough results. Environmental factors for the creative environment are applicable to the innovative environment and

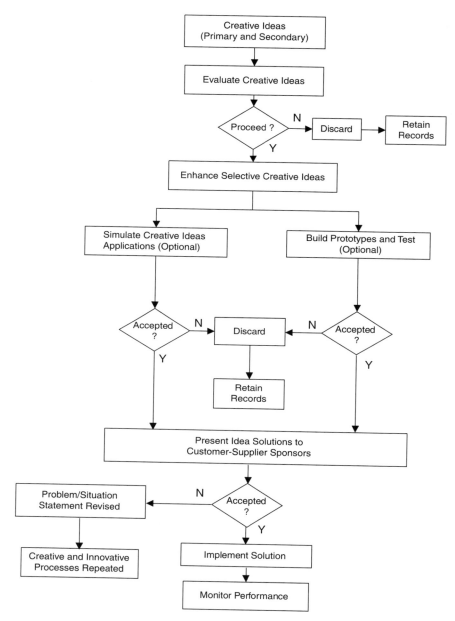

Figure 6.1. Innovative process.

Table 6.1. Creative and innovative processes comparison.

	Creative	Innovative
Team involvement	Y	Y
Define new ideas	Y	N
Propose best ideas for innovation	Y	N
Modify proposed ideas	N	Y
Simulation of usefulness	N	Y
Determine risk	N	Y
Build and test prototypes	N	Y
Presentation to sponsors	N	Y
Implement solution	N	Y
Monitor performance	N	Y

when adjusted for the customer-supplier innovation team become: sufficient resources, freedom to explore, open communication, trust, and a commitment to succeed (Amabile 1996). It is the responsibility of the co-leaders to guide the team to its full potential.

To gain a global competitive advantage and to sustain this advantage will require product, service, and process breakthroughs. It is the innovation of products, processes, marketing, and management that make a company a leader in the global market. An innovation team must keep these four areas in mind from a system's standpoint when using the innovation process. The reasoning is that a system linkage exists and the optimization of a single area will create a cause and effect relationship of a lesser value with the other areas. A careful operational balance of these factors is required to deliver the expected results.

WORK ENVIRONMENT INFLUENCE

An important but sometimes overlooked factor for the innovative work environment is the stimuli acquired from exposure to ideas and influences outside a person's immediate field. One company with an outstanding reputation for supporting environments that spawn innovative products and processes is 3M. In this regard, microreplication is a major technological breakthrough for 3M. It provides an innovative portal for future processes and products.

It is found in products as diverse as overhead projector lenses, reflective sheeting for highways signs, abrasives, and computer mouse pads. 3M™ Trizact™ Abrasive belts (*sandpaper* to the general public) represent an excellent innovative work environment example. It's impressive to note that 3M's leadership in the abrasives market for more than 90 years isn't grinding to a halt. In fact, 3M's innovative spirit is responsible for reinventing not only a new abrasive process, but also sandpaper and other abrasive products.

It's not surprising that the Trizact Abrasives story begins with two separate yet connected inquiries. Microreplication technology is well known throughout 3M. Creating additional new-to-the-world products with this technology requires inquisitive minds. A senior technical specialist in the Abrasive Systems Division was looking for ways to improve aviation fuel consumption by sanding groves into airplane wings. He asked the question "why not microreplicated abrasives?" At the same time, a process engineer, at the 3M Central Research Process Technology Laboratory, was working to link microreplication technology to abrasives. These two individuals joined forces to find an innovative solution. The process engineer was evaluating methods for using light to cure resins. Traditional coated abrasives required large curing ovens that consumed significant energy to evaporate water and/or solvents and cure the resins. Light curing eliminates the need for both solvents and ovens and greatly speeds up the process. As it turned out, light curing provided the technology that enables the manufacture of structured abrasive products. A process was developed to deposit a mixture of mineral and resin onto a backing—such as cloth—to form precise microscopic pyramids. Samples were created. These samples were used not only to produce grooves, but also very smooth surfaces, e.g., polishing silicon wafers.

The success with the exploratory Trizact Abrasives samples was reported to 3M senior management. A green light was given to move the innovative process forward. An internal customer-supplier innovation team was formed with people from various 3M laboratories. In structure, the team had a dedicated manager, can-do team leaders, and unflagging corporate support. The team interactions were one of unhesitating sharing of diverse technological resources across internal boundaries.

An outside facilitator was used for the team-building process. The facilitator was brought back at stages in the innovative process to keep the team momentum going. Meetings were held monthly with the full team to discuss what had been achieved and what remained to be done.

Team planning and idea thinking used Post-it™ notes on a large white board. Individual Post-it™ notes were arranged and rearranged to create a plan. This same approach was used for brainstorming of ideas and other creative thinking methods. The plan was refined periodically and changes highlighted. This made the plan very visible to the team.

The team started its effort in 1990. It faced the task to invent the production process and build a plant. Trizact Abrasives were introduced to customers in 1995. Thanks to team members for their curiosity and innovative spirit, sandpaper will never be the same. It's better! (Norausky 1999C).

CREATIVE IDEA TRANSFER

The process used by the team to accept creative ideas for the innovative process is as follows:

- Ideas pass a basic screening process at the creative stage.
- The problem/situation statement is reviewed to ensure the statement still applies. A blank worksheet and completed example are provided in Appendix E.1 and E.2.
- The strengths, weaknesses and requirement for additional information and data are identified and discussed for each idea. A worksheet is provided in Appendix E.3.
- Team members rank the ideas within the primary idea group and within the secondary group. Care is exercised so as not to artificially reject a good idea. Ranking of an idea begins with an overall impression of the idea as a solution. This takes into consideration the strengths and weaknesses of the idea. A scale of low, medium, or high is used. A consensus position is reached for the overall impression conveyed by each idea. As with the creative process and the evaluation of creative ideas, value represents the ability of the idea to satisfy the problem/situation statement. It

Table 6.2. Value-cost matrix.

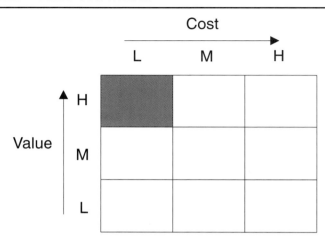

provides a reference for comparison. Cost, performance, quality, dependability, life of the solution, projected return on investment, market impact, extent solution is leading edge, time to implement solution, customer acceptance, and risk are rated for each idea relative to value. These factors are rated as low, medium, or high. A consensus position on the rating is reach for each idea.

• A record is kept for each idea and the associated rating information.

An example of a Value-Cost Matrix is shown in Table 6.2. Guidance is provided in Table 6.3 for rating value and the comparison factors. Generally, the rating levels of low, medium, and high shown in Table 6.3 are considered ideal. To make breakthroughs, the risk level should be medium to high. Otherwise, the solution may not provide a competitive advantage. The team must use judgement for accepting a solution when the ratings deviate from those shown in Table 6.3.

There are problems/situations where low cost may not be the acceptable screening factor. For example, in terms of safety and environmental concerns, higher cost may be tolerated and accepted in order to responsibly resolve a problem/situation.

Table 6.3.   Innovative idea rating guidance (ideal).

	Overall Impression	Cost	Performance	Quality	Dependability	Life of Solution	Projected ROI	Market Impact	Leading Edge	Time to Implement	Customer Acceptance	Risk
H	H	L	H	H	H	H	H	H	H	L	H	L
Value M												
L												

In high technology industries, a *fast track* solution with a higher cost may lead to a significant competitive advantage. The urgency of getting the product or service to the market as fast as possible in order to generate very high revenues while beating out the competition creates a unique justification for a high cost solution. With a low cost solution, the time for implementation may be so long that the value of the technology is lost as competitive leverage.

INNOVATIVE TECHNIQUES

Team members must now think in terms of the practical aspects of newly created ideas and the process to implement these ideas as solutions.

Team members, like experts in wine testing who wash out their mouths before tasting a different wine, must wash out their mental processes that created ideas in favor of the process for serious evaluation leading to solution implementation. This requires the application of technical and business techniques.

The TRIZ technique begun in the creative process continues to refine and produce solutions that can be implemented. The innovative techniques coupled with the creative techniques provide a solution system. The customer-supplier innovation team must use judgement as to the innovative techniques that are used. Innovative techniques for the most part represent a continuation of the techniques used in the creative process. These techniques are identified as: Brainstorming, TRIZ, Force Field Analysis and Free Association.

The innovative process involves a combination of technical and business techniques. The same technical techniques used in the creative process are used appropriately in the innovative process. Business techniques become important in the innovative process because of the need to provide realistic solutions that can be implemented and solve not only technical aspects of the problem, but also address business issues that especially impact the bottom line in less than acceptable manner. Business techniques involve but are not limited to: 1. Risk Analysis, 2. Trade-off Analysis, 3. Return on Investment (ROI).

PRESENTING THE INNOVATIVE SOLUTION

The team co-leaders are responsible for keeping the sponsors informed on the progress of the team. In essence, the sponsors should never be surprised. Depending on the sponsors and the associated cultures, the team's selling job may or may not be difficult.

A presentation to sponsors should contain major topics shown in Figure 6.2. All team members should be included to give some part of the presentation. The presentation should convey the fact that the team was thorough in using the creative and innovative processes. Team confidence must be high in order to make a successful presentation. A set of questions expected to be asked by the sponsors should be defined and answers prepared for verbal and/or written responses, as needed, during the presentation. A dry run of the presentation should be conducted. A critique should be made of the material presented and the team member's delivery. A worksheet is provided in Appendix C.4. Above all, the intent of the presentation is to accurately portray data and information about the proposed solution so the sponsors can make a responsible decision whether or not to proceed with implementation.

Topical Outline

◊ Introduction

◊ Team objective

◊ Team membership

◊ Operational period

◊ Problem/solution statement

◊ Brief explanation of approach used by the team

◊ Creative process

◊ Innovative process

◊ Proposed solution

◊ Technical, financial, market benefits

◊ Risks

◊ Implementation time

◊ Resources required for implementation

◊ Recommendation

◊ Request for decision

Figure 6.2. Presentation topical outline.

TEAM TRAINING FOR INNOVATIVE PROCESS

In addition to the basic training received for creative process, team members need the following education and training courses for the innovative process:

- Business Economics and Financials
- Risk Analysis
- Trade-Off Analysis
- Quality Function Deployment

A brief description of each course is covered as follows:

Business Economics and Financials. Basic treatment of economic principles and the relationship with markets, tactics, and strategies are covered. Financial principles for running a business are presented.

Risk Analysis. Offers the process to identify, categorize, and reduce risk associated with products, services, processes, and systems.

Trade-Off Analysis. Process to evaluate multiple factors and the impact on products, services, processes, and systems.

Quality Function Deployment (QFD). Takes the *voice of the customer* and evaluates the impact of various functions, e.g. marketing, manufacturing, engineering, procurement to reach a collective position required to satisfy the *voice of the customer.*

TAKING RISKS

The team determines that the best solution for the problem/situation involves a radical breakthrough. The solution is classified as high risk. If the team stops at this point and doesn't further evaluate the other selection factors, then the team isn't extending itself to mitigate or eliminate risk. A great solution may be lost. The key to the team taking risks relative to selecting solutions begins with the steps shown for the innovation risk process in Figure 6.3.

1. Establish the Environment
   - Understand the environment in which the risk exists.

Innovation Risk Process

1. Establish the environment
2. Identify
3. Analyze
4. Evaluate and prioritize
5. Treat the risk
6. Monitor and review

Figure 6.3. Innovation risk process.

- Identify strategic and operational issues like political, legal and financial circumstances, and market or industry conditions, whether key personnel are involved in the purchase.
- Be aware of how the risk relates to the problem/situation statement.
- Identify the stakeholders.
- Determine what and who is affected by the risk.
- Define the successful outcomes required for mitigation or elimination of the risk.

2. Identify the Risks
   - What can happen? How and why does it happen? The objective of this step is to develop a comprehensive, documented list of all potential risks.
   - Consider the risks from the perspective of all stakeholders.
   - What problems have the stakeholders experienced in the past with this type of risk?
   - Think about the risk impact over time associated with the product, service, process, or system relative to, for instance, aging, obsolescence, life cycle, cost.
   - Identify the risk categories: technical, financial, human, commercial, and other categories that impact the proposed solution.

- The team can identify risks by several methods such as: developing checklists on the key features of the solution, brainstorming, surveys, drawing on past experience, SWOT analysis (identifying the strengths, weaknesses, opportunities and threats), flowcharting, and scenario analysis.

3. Analyze the Risks

- What is the likelihood of the risks occurring?
- What are the consequences of the risks occurring?
- For each identified risk, determine its consequences and its probability. Combine these estimates to give you an overall estimated level of risk. Identify any existing controls used to manage this risk (such as purchasing procedures or internal audit). Evaluate the risks in the context of these existing controls.

When considering consequences of a risk, think about:

- How critical is the outcome of the solution?
- What, who, and how many are affected by the risk?

When considering probability of a risk occurring, think about:

- The frequency of exposure to the risk. As the frequency of exposure to the risk increases, the probability is higher (usually).

A range of qualitative and quantitative methods are available to help you analyze consequences and probabilities of risk. One common qualitative method is to use experience, good judgement and a simple scale of intensity/severity. For example, consequences and probability can be defined using simple rating scales like High, Medium or Low; Highly Likely to Very Unlikely; or numeric scales 1–5.

Try to avoid subjective judgements. Be objective in determining your ratings of risks. Ask regularly, "Would an independent person reach the same conclusion?"

Start with a simple qualitative method of analysis to get a general indication of risk and to do the initial screening and then if necessary, use quantitative analysis for more specific analysis. Quantitative analysis may be necessary for complex and/or high value risks.

Qualitative methods (use descriptive/word scales):

Past records/experience, market research, product information/brochures-industry practice and standards, specialist/expert judgements surveys, interviews, experiments/tests, event tree analysis.

Quantitative methods (use numerical information to arrive at percentages, dollar values or numeric values):

Cost benefit analysis.

4. Evaluate and Prioritize the Risks
   - What is the priority of the risks?
   - What is the acceptable level of risk?
   - Which risks will be the focus for treatment action?

From the information obtained in steps 2 and 3, arrange the listing of risks in priority order and decide which are acceptable to unacceptable. This will allow you to determine priorities for treatment of the risks.

To determine the acceptability of each risk, compare it against the risk assessment criteria defined in step 1.

As the priority moves to medium and high, the team needs to determine the acceptability of the solution. When probability and consequence are both low, it may be possible to accept risks without further action, or implement simple standards procedures.

There is a degree of judgement involved in determining the level of risk.

5. Treat the Risk
   - What can be done to minimize risk?
   - What resources are needed? What measures are needed to monitor the levels of risk?
   - Identify the range of options for treating the risk and evaluate those options. Prepare a risk treatment plan to support implementation of the solution.
   - The documented treatment plan should identify who is accountable for which responsibilities, schedules, expected outcome of treatments, budgets, and performance criteria.

Options for Treating Risk:

Accept It:

It may be possible to accept the risk.
When?
When the consequences/probability are low. When it is the most cost-effective treatment or there are clear benefits.
After other treatment options have reduced the risk to an acceptable level. When the risk can be controlled.

Avoid It:

When?
When the risks are considered too high, unmanageable, or too costly and there are other ways to achieve the solution.
As a point of consideration, it can often be more costly to avoid the risk, than to choose other options for treating the risk.

Reduce It:

When?
When a solution presents a high risk but also a good opportunity, for example, introduction of new technology. A combination of risk treatments may be necessary.

6. Monitor and Review

If the proposed solution is accepted and then implemented, the team must remain vigilant that the risk doesn't jeopardize the solution from being successful.
Are new risks arising?
Keep developing risk management *thinking.*

TEAM PROGRESS

Though the creative and innovative processes are generally viewed as free from pressure, indicators for progress need to be established and understood by the team before starting the innovative process. An example of measures, metrics and measurements are shown in Table 6.4.

Table 6.4. Team progress (example).

	Idea	Idea	Idea	Idea
Measure	Selection	Enhancement	Simulation total	Simulation success
Metric Measurement	Accepted 3	Number 6	Number 5	Number 3

	Idea	Idea	Management
Measure	Prototype	Prototype success	Schedule
Metric Measurement	Number 2	Number 1	On-Schedule Yes

INNOVATIVE PROCESS TIME COMPRESSION

When a customer-supplier innovation team is formed, the sponsors define an end date for expected results. This sets a time constraint for team performance.

Time compression of the innovative process can occur in one of two ways. First, none of the creative ideas submitted to the innovative process offer acceptable solutions, and second the end date is changed to shorten the time for expected results due to increased competition or a combination of other market-driven factors.

In evaluating the ideas that are submitted, it may be concluded that none of the submitted ideas are acceptable. In this instance, the creative process is reactivated and additional ideas are sought. Even though the time pressure exists, care is taken not to contaminate the creative process by not following the steps that are proven as successful steps.

RETURN TO THE CREATIVE PROCESS

The time pressure is increased when the team must re-enter the creative process to generate new ideas. These steps are usually followed:

1. Understand reasons why submitted creative ideas were not accepted.

2. Review the problem/solution statement to ensure that it is still valid.
3. Define an end date for completing the creative process.
4. Relax; clear the mind and focus. Don't panic mentally because of the shortened time frame. Consider the shortened time frame as a challenge to perform with excellence.
5. Avoid all distractions.
6. Use one or more of the creative idea generating techniques.
7. Evaluate the creative ideas, select, and submit ideas to the innovation process.

In most circumstances time for the return to the creative process can be shortened by 50 percent or more because the team is familiar with the creative process and the problem/solution statement.

INNOVATIVE PROCESS: SECOND TIME

With newly submitted creative ideas, the team can now concentrate on returning to the innovative process. Steps will involve:

1. Determine that the problem/solution statement remains valid.
2. Acknowledge and commit to the end date for innovative results.
3. Engage the steps in the innovative process. Time may only exist for simulations and not for building and testing prototypes.
4. Increase communication with customer and supplier sponsors to report status.
5. Provide innovative solutions with emphasis, as necessary, with regards to risks and shortcomings in view of the shortened time frame.

WEB SITES FOR INNOVATION

Use the Internet and search engines such as: www.altavista.com, www.metacrawler.com, or www.yahoo.com. Some key words or phases to use: innovative process, innovative best practices, innovative training, 3M innovation, innovation chronicles, glass innovation, automotive innovation.

Several web sites of interest are:

http://www.thinksmart.com. The Innovation network is a dynamic group of people dedicated to improving their organizations through the powerful use of innovation, creativity and collaboration skills.

http://www.pbs.org/nova. Nova offers new ideas and innovations to stimulate further thinking.

http://www.corbis.com/leonardo97. The Corbis Leonardo da Vinci profile details his intellectual curiosity and ability to integrate ideas across disciplines.

http://www-east.elsevier.com. Sample information for The Journal of Product Innovation Management. This publication is dedicated to the advancement of management practice in all functions involved in the total process of product innovation.

http://www.ia-usa.org. Center for Innovation in Biomedical Technology web site with many connecting links.

http://www.triz-journal.com. An excellent on-line publication with many articles on TRIZ. Articles can be downloaded or printed.

http://www.innovationcenter.org. The Oregon Innovation Center is a not-for-profit corporation funded by area business, public sources, and entrepreneurs to help technology-based start-ups succeed.

LESSONS LEARNED

1. Mental shift needed from the creative process to the innovative process. This must be at the conscious level.

2. Breakthrough thinking is required to better ensure innovative solutions provide a competitive advantage and that the advantage is sustained for a reasonable period of time. Kaizen with small incremental achievement is no longer considered a world-class approach.

3. Factors that stifle innovation must be identified immediately and action taken to eliminate these factors.

4. The team co-leaders must ensure environmental factors are satisfied. This avoids the situation of the team losing a sense of purpose.

5. Team members must be honest and open with each other and be willing to support consensus positions.

6. The team needs to practice the presentation of the proposed selected solution to the sponsors. This contributes to a smooth and well-formulated presentation needed for responsible decision making.

7. What gets done, gets measured. The progress of an innovation team isn't any exception. The team's progress needs to be followed with realistic measures, metrics, and measurements.

8. Team members require training to function effectively in the innovative process.

9. When an urgent situation occurs, the innovative process time usually is compressed. Team members must be aware of the steps that change when the time is compressed.

10. Lessons learned regarding the innovative process applied to the customer-supplier innovation team are covered.

11. The reader is presented with a series of questions regarding the innovative process applied to the customer-supplier innovation team.

SUMMARY

1. Innovation requires the act to use a newly created idea.

2. Innovation offers a competitive advantage. World-class companies such as General Electric and 3M are not only very outspoken about innovation, their results provide evidence. With rapid change and global competition, gone is the comfort of working for incremental improvements. Enter the need for continuous innovation that produces breakthrough results.

3. The common techniques used for the creative process also apply to the innovative process. These techniques are brainstorming, force analysis, TRIZ and Free Association. Business techniques, for instance, risk analysis, trade-off analysis and return on investment (ROI) are added since the solution must satisfy not only technical, but also business factors.

4. The innovative process is vulnerable to factors that stifle the process. Recognizing these factors enables the team to take corrective action.

5. The innovative process is described by means of a flow chart in Figure 6.1.

6. Critical to the team's success is the innovative work environment. These environmental factors are: sufficient resources, freedom to explore, open communication, trust, and a commitment to succeed.

7. The acceptance of a creative idea for innovative processing is described in Table 6.2, Value-Cost Matrix, and Table 6.3, Innovative Idea Rating Guidance (Ideal).

8. The team selects the solution. Now the team must make a presentation to the sponsors. A topical outline is covered with suggestions for preparing the presentation as well as a form for critiquing speakers during a dry-run session.

9. Training of the team for the innovative process is covered. Primarily, this involves education and training concerning

business economics and financials, risk analysis, trade-off analysis, and Quality Function Deployment (QFD).

10. The progress of the team needs to be measured to ensure results are available according to schedule. An example for measures, metrics, and measurements are contained in Table 6.4.

11. Random situations may create the urgency for time compression of the innovative process. A procedure is described to best handle this situation.

12. Web sites for innovation are covered. Surfing these sites will lead to other site discoveries.

13. Lessons learned from team operating within the innovative process are presented.

14. The reader is presented with a series of questions to answer relative to using the innovative process in his or her organization

QUESTIONS

1. What is innovation?

2. What process does the team use to be innovative?

3. What work environment is needed for innovation?

4. How does the team select the creative idea(s) for the innovative process?

5. What are the innovative techniques?

6. How does the innovative process work?

7. Can the innovative process be time compressed?

8. What approving authority is needed to proceed within the innovative process?

9. What process does the team use to sell the innovation(s) as the solution to the stated requirement? How does the process work?

10. What training does the team need to best participate in the innovative process?

11. What are examples at the various stages of the innovative process?

12. What types of exercises can the member and the team do in order to engage in the innovative process?

13. What are the lessons learned from using the innovative process in a team setting?

14. What happens when the *team* or some other source requires a schedule for innovative output?

15. What are the web sites for innovation?

16. How do world-class customer-supplier innovation teams use the innovative process?

17. What are factors that stifle the innovative process?

18. How can these stifling factors be eliminated/overcome?

19. Why does the innovative process work?

20. When does the team take *risks* with innovative solutions? How is this done?

21. What is the daily routine for the team to exercise the innovative process?

22. What measures are used to determine successful progress?

Operating the Team  7

"When you have got an elephant by the hind legs and he is trying to run away, it is best to let him run."

Abraham Lincoln

"Who rides a tiger cannot dismount."

Chinese Proverb

"Take my assets—but leave me my organization and in five years I'll have it all back."

Alfred P. Sloan

OPERATIONAL PROCESS

Launching the Team

The operational process begins once the matter of assessment scoring and Innovative Focus Quotients are understood by team members and any issues resolved. The sponsors activate the team by providing clear vision and mission statements, objectives, and expectations. The team is launched to do its job. Co-leaders are used to manage both the team and project. Each sponsor designates a co-leader. It should be noted that when a project is internal to a company and both the customer and supplier come from internal organizations, then a single leader is

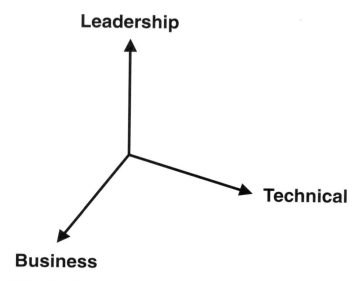

Figure 7.1. Co-leader traits.

appointed. Team leaders must not only possess the traits previously covered in chapter 2, but also leadership abilities and a business viewpoint. These two traits will bring balance to the team and better ensure technical as well as a leadership and business focus in pursuit of the objectives, Figure 7.1. These individuals are trained and are expected to support each other for the team to reach its objectives and full potential.

Operational Process Model

An operational process model is shown in Figure 7.2. Team management and project management are applied to the creative and innovative processes to produce intended results. For the customer-supplier innovation team to be successful, team management is separated from the traditional project management format. This separation highlights the importance of managing the team and better ensures attention to the team making the project work successful. *In the traditional project management process, managing the team is included as a sub-process.* Further, it is recognized that the customer-supplier innovation team must have the freedom to be creative and achieve innovative solutions.

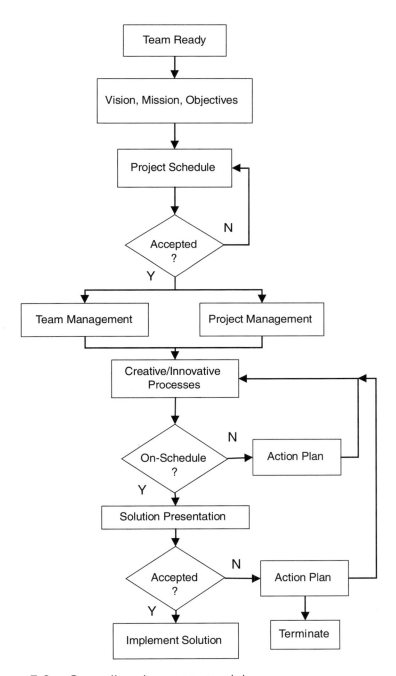

Figure 7.2. Operational process model.

On the other hand, it is essential that the project be managed like any other business undertaking. However, the project management approach is low key, and the rigor of traditional project management is generally transparent to team members. *For example, the co-leaders monitor cost relative to the budget. They have the responsibility to keep on-track and not exceed the budget.*

PROJECT MANAGEMENT

Phases

The tried and proven project management approach is used for operating the customer-supplier innovation team. Project management involves five phases: 1. define, 2. plan, 3. execute, 4. monitor and control, and 5. close.

Define. Project sponsors define the vision, mission, objectives, expectations, and *end date* for the project. Also, the sponsors provide a problem/situation statement, outline preliminary resources, identify project assumptions and potential risks. The team co-leaders are appointed by the sponsors. A worksheet and example are provided in Appendix F.1 and F.2 respectively.

Plan. The team co-leaders are responsible for the project plan. A top level, *first-cut* project plan is prepared. The team co-leaders discuss this plan with the team, refine as necessary, and proceed to prepare a practical working level plan. The intent in this process is not to create a detail plan that will become burdensome. Quite the contrary, the plan should be detailed sufficiently to provide guidance for accomplishing the project assigned to the team.

Execute. Plan the work, work the plan. The co-leaders use the plan as a guide in moving through the creative process and then into the innovative process. Generally, the team should not be bothered with the specifics of the plan. This is especially true while working in the creative phase.

Monitor and Control. As effort is being expended on the project, the co-leaders should be monitoring the costs versus the budget.

Measures, metrics, and measurements enable the co-leaders to realistically establish the state of the project relative to the plan. Adjustments can then be made to better control the direction that the effort should be focused to move forward for intended results.

Close. The project is closed when the *end date* is reached. Closure for the team occurs when the innovative solution is implemented. It is a time for the team to celebrate. The team decides on the manner for celebration.

Boundary Conditions

Traditional project management involves three variable boundary conditions namely: time, cost, and performance. Project environments are dynamic and these boundary conditions need to be balanced in an agreed to manner since each condition is independent of the other conditions. Results define the outcome of how well these three variables were managed. For the customer-supplier innovation team the boundary conditions become cost, time, and innovation. This is shown in Figure 7.3. Boundary condition measures are shown in Figure 7.4 as budget, schedule, and solutions. A change to one or more of the variables will cause a

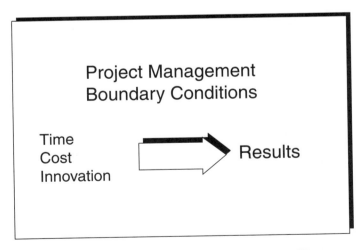

Figure 7.3.   Project management boundary conditions.

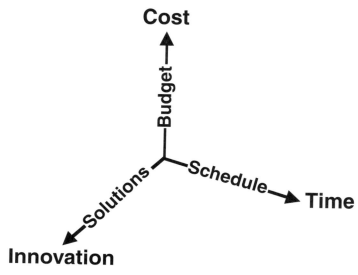

Figure 7.4. Boundary conditions and measures.

change in the other variables. For example, if time and funds for a project are reduced, this could limit the innovative process and subsequent innovative solutions. Results may not meet the sponsors' expectations.

Co-Leaders Check List

A human experience . . . forgetting to attend to a detail when under pressure, just simply omitted, not part of the routine and/or when a routine is broken. A good method to help prevent this from happening is the use of a checklist. After all, aircraft pilots use a checklist. The landing gear is always put down on the approach to landing. A checklist to help the co-leaders manage a project is provided in Appendix F.3. As co-leaders gain experience with a project, it is suggested that they add items to the check list. This process makes for an even more valuable checklist of items for future projects. A good habit to pursue.

Project Schedule

The objectives, expectations, problem/situation statement, preliminary resources, and end date provide input for formulating a project schedule. The co-leaders create a top level Gantt Chart. The co-leaders and team refine the top level Gantt Chart for operational purposes. This chart is intended not to constrain the creative/innovative processes but to set milestone targets to better ensure results are available when needed.

Approval of the schedule rests with the team. The team uses a consensus process to reach an approval decision. A provision exists for the team to revise the schedule as circumstances warrant. Sponsors are only concerned that the *end date* is met with a satisfactory innovative solution(s). The team must obtain approval from the sponsors to extend the *end date.*

Co-leaders communicate the project status to the sponsors with weekly reports. At the beginning of the project, sponsors agreed not to interfere with the management of the project. The co-leaders are responsible to stay on-track per the schedule.

Co-leaders monitor progress against the schedule. Generally, this requires judgment on the part of the co-leaders since activities and outcomes generally are somewhat fluid within the creative/innovative processes. This fluidity should not prevent a prognosis as to status and a corresponding projection on progress versus time. The mindset of *make the plan, work the plan* better ensures even in creative and innovative environments that a higher probability exists to produce results. One method that has proven successful with customer-supplier innovation teams is for the co-leaders to use small, definable work packages. Co-leaders plan a creative/innovative session by defining deliverables at the end of the session. Once the session is conducted, it will be apparent whether or not the deliverables were realized. The status of deliverables will enable the co-leaders to make a *judgement call* as to the extent of the impact on the project schedule. By using the small work package approach and defining deliverables throughout the course of the project, the co-leaders will be in a excellent position to not only monitor but control activities to keep the project on schedule. This process is shown in Figure 7.5.

If a project falls behind schedule just a little, the co-leaders must quickly identify the problem and deal with it immediately. The key for the co-leaders to complete the schedule on time, on budget, and with solutions that can be implemented is to begin the project

```
            Project Monitor and Control

      1. Use small work packages
      2. Define deliverables
      3. Compare expected versus actual deliverables
      4. Determine schedule impact
      5. Define corrective actions, as needed
      6. Implement corrective actions
```

Figure 7.5.   Project monitor and control.

on-track and stay on track. As the completion of the project is approached and the project is off schedule, it will be almost impossible to catch up and meet the sponsors' end date with required deliverables, for example, solutions that can be implemented.

Communication

Co-leaders are responsible for keeping the lines of communication open with the team as well as the sponsors. Some of the best communication can occur informally and unexpectedly with team members. Co-leaders need to listen and watch for signs of both accomplishment and concerns.

All information is communicated simultaneously to team members via e-mail and/or team meetings. Action items are assigned as needed. The principle of *no surprises* is followed.

Team
- Meetings
  - Formal (frequency: weekly)
  - Informal (frequency: spontaneously)
- E-mail
- Reports (verbal, written)
- Creative sessions
- Innovative sessions

Sponsors
- Weekly status reports (verbal, written)
- E-mail
- Milestone presentations (information only)
- Presentation of proposed solution

Creative Process

Project management of the creative process is conducted in a manner not to stifle creativity. This means that the co-leaders must manage the creative process by ensuring the team is provided with the motivation, resources, facilities, and environment to be creative.

The team should not be reminded constantly about schedule, budget, and output. Though the team is accountable to deliver results, the co-leaders are responsible for leadership to inspire team members and keep the team motivated.

The co-leaders plan and select a creative technique to use depending on the problem/situation, phase (for example, just getting started or mature) and required output. This does not mean that the process is rigid. It simply indicates that an initial direction is chosen.

Innovative Process

In the innovative process, the team becomes more aware and involved with business factors, for example, cost, time, and solutions. Co-leaders are required to begin a process of steering team members to evaluate creative ideas from the standpoint that ideas satisfy the items set forth for an innovative solution (See Tables 6.2 and 6.3.)

Also, from a schedule standpoint, solutions are expected and the time frame is shorter than allowed for the creative process. Of course, the time allowed for the creative and innovative process can be allocated as needed depending on the complexity of the problem/situation statement.

A contingency plan is defined by the co-leaders in the event that innovative solutions do not emerge from the creative process. This is strictly a back-up action since a positive theme of success is communicated from the start of the project.

Documentation

A considerable amount of data and information is generated in Figure 7.2, Operational Process. The co-leaders are responsible for a process that ensures records are made, stored, and can be retrieved by all members of the team.

A person outside of the team is usually assigned as the *record keeper.* This involves attending all meetings to record the data and information and to provide a database that is accessible to all team members.

Costs must be documented and tracked. Though this data is available to all team members, it is essentially compiled for the co-leaders. Depending on the complexity of the project, a person outside of the team would be assigned to keep track of the costs. On small projects this can easily be done by the co-leaders.

Project Risk

Project risk as impacted by the time, cost, and innovation-variable-boundary conditions needs to be determined by the co-leaders. This is determined by the co-leaders evaluating the schedule, budget, and solutions for a current point in time relative to what should exist for the same point in time. Risk should be designated as low, medium, and high. A guidance chart is shown in Figure 7.6.

TEAM MANAGEMENT

You manage the project and you manage the team. As stated earlier in this chapter, traditional project management includes managing the team. For the sake of providing greater attention to the team, especially for the creative and innovative processes, it is appropriate to break the team out separately and create the need for a simultaneous balance with the project. This is done with good cross-linkage between the team and the project since the team is small (for example usually eight people maximum) and members possess a unified sense of team purpose.

Team management addresses:

- Schedule
- Communication

```
Project Risk Levels


High:       Schedule = 21% to 40% behind
            Budget = 21% to 30% over budget
            Solutions = poor prospect

Medium:     Schedule = 6% to 20% behind
            Budget = 6% to 20% over budget
            Solutions = fair prospect

Low:        Schedule = On to 5% behind
            Budget = 2% to 5% over budget
            Solutions = good prospect
```

Figure 7.6.   Project risk level.

- Morale Issues
- Conflict Resolution
- Benchmarking
- Patents
- Creative Process
- Innovative Process
- Celebration
- Results

Schedule

It seems very contradictory to address a schedule in managing the team for creative and innovative purposes. Schedules suggest boundaries and expected outputs. The reality of the business world, especially the global business world, requires dynamic change on a continual basis. Overlaying the need for the team to comply with a schedule doesn't create a barrier but actually acts as a motivator for the creative and innovative processes. It is a motivator only to the extent that the co-leaders manage the team in a manner that acknowledges the schedule and its importance but doesn't allow the schedule to become

---

Team and Schedule

1. Make the schedule visible but not a focus
2. Clearly state deliverables expected from the team
3. Provide encouragement and resources
4. Never make the schedule problems an issue
5. Maintain an active *freedom to discover* environment

Figure 7.7. Team and schedule.

the focus, rather only the motivator. The team is kept informed about the schedule and progress but the co-leaders avoid making the schedule *an issue*. It is a task for the co-leaders to take action to keep on schedule. Team members are accountable to participate in the creative and innovative processes and apply their talents and energy to produce required deliverables. When the team is managed successfully, the schedule never becomes an issue.

The co-leaders need to follow the guidance shown in Figure 7.7 for managing the team according to a schedule.

Communication

Open communication must exist at all times. Co-leaders are responsible to provide an environment where team members are free to discuss any aspect of the project both positive and negative in the spirit of honest inquiry. Further, team members are encouraged to talk about ideas that may deviate from the norm and especially, their area of technical expertise. For example, a team member wanted to discuss an idea that he didn't have the depth of technical background but felt the general concept of the idea offered merit. He was encouraged to continue a discussion and fellow team members who possessed expertise provided technical insight to better explain the idea. As it turned out, this idea lead to the innovative solution known as water based paint. The problem was to eliminate the solvent carrier in paint and thus, eliminate an air emission issue.

Weekly meetings are held with team members to provide a forum for issues of general interest and to cover the project's status. Team members assigned investigative task take this opportunity to report on their findings. The team is able to collectively gauge the status of the project and what's left to be done. Co-leaders keep the meeting upbeat regardless of pressing issues.

Informal settings contribute to the most productive conversations. The office space is arranged with a sense of openness rather than cubicles so that the excitement of conversation charges the atmosphere. There are closed offices for situations that may require isolation.

Morale Issues

The same principle is applied to morale as to schedule slip. Co-leaders must identify a morale problem and deal with the problem immediately. For example, a team member regarded as highly productive with an outgoing personality was observed one day to be very argumentative in several conversations. A co-leader invited this team member to join him for a cup of coffee. After a brief conversation, the co-leader learned that the team member had started to take a different medication for his allergy condition. His reaction to the medication was abnormal. The team member called his doctor and was instructed to change the medication immediately as he was experiencing a psychotic reaction. Valuable learning occurred for the co-leaders, team member, and the team . . . don't hesitate to find out what's wrong when attitudes and behaviors change. Put a root cause correction in place.

There are situations where the morale of the entire team is affected. For example, the physical environment that the team is expected to work in may be sub-standard and not conducive to creative thought and activities. Co-leaders must make the necessary changes. After all, the co-leaders are the champions for the team. They must be willing to act as leaders to get resources

```
┌─────────────────────────────────────────┐
│                                          │
│            Morale Guidelines             │
│                                          │
│   1. Be vigilant and make observations   │
│   2. Be supportive and listen            │
│   3. Calmly determine root cause(s)      │
│   4. Implement corrective action(s)      │
│   5. Learn from the experience           │
│                                          │
└─────────────────────────────────────────┘
```

Figure 7.8. Morale guidelines.

from the sponsors. In an extreme case, they must be willing to state that the project cannot go forth without the needed resources. If resources are not provided, they must be willing to resign from the project. No less is expected from such leaders. Morale guidelines for co-leaders are shown in Figure 7.8.

Conflict Resolution

Members of the team were chosen to be diverse yet compatible with regard to creativity and innovation. Strong dissenting opinions are to be expected and, in fact, encouraged. Constructive discourse represents the incubator for breakthrough thinking and discovery. Unless such discourse is managed properly, conflict can result. Conflict is considered a negative element with the team. A listing of potential conflict arrangements is presented in Figure 7.9.

So a conflict exists. What to do? In the majority of conflicts, the co-leaders are expected to resolve the conflict. An accepted approach to resolving the conflict involves the co-leader(s) 1. treating the other party with respect, 2. listening to understand and 3. expressing their views, needs, and feelings in an assertive manner. Once an agreement is reached, a corrective action is implemented. An example of a conflict may simply be over the shared use of a high-speed computer, for example a Cray 900-19 supercomputer needed to simulate real time material deformations. The two team members cannot agree on a usage schedule since each person regards their use as more important than the other person's use.

```
┌─────────────────────────────────────────┐
│                                          │
│         Conflict Arrangements            │
│                                          │
│     1. Individual vs. other team members │
│     2. Individual vs. another team member│
│     3. Team divided against itself       │
│     4. Co-leader(s) vs. team (part or full)│
│     5. Co-leader vs. co-leader           │
│     6. Team vs. sponsor                  │
│                                          │
└─────────────────────────────────────────┘
```

Figure 7.9. Conflict arrangements.

Benchmarking

Seeking ideas from other sources outside the realm of the customer and supplier can provide a new source to stimulate thinking about products, services, processes, and systems. From experience, benchmarking should not be used for the creative and innovative processes until all other means of generating ideas and refining these ideas are exhausted. The reason is that benchmarking could narrow the focus rather than expand the view. If used in the beginning, and the first product, service, process, or system that is examined appears feasible as a potential solution, there can be a tendency to stop and go no further. To do so, obviously limits a greater range of possibilities. Co-leaders must use benchmarking wisely and not fall victim to "We found the solution; let's not proceed any further."

The benchmarking process involves nine steps:

1. Do the homework before seeking solutions. This means understand the problem/situation and the parameters that a solution must be able to satisfy.
2. Search and identify potential sources to benchmark.
3. Prepare a list of questions before making contact with a source.

4. Be prepared to offer an exchange of information or some other benefit that makes the benchmarking beneficial to both parties.
5. Conduct the benchmarking study at the source.
6. After the study at the source, evaluate the learning obtained.
7. Apply the learning to the team's project.
8. Repeat a benchmarking study with another source. Adjust the benchmarking questions based on previous benchmarking studies.
9. Apply the learning to the team's project.

Patents

The patent process, unless made visible, may be forgotten in the creative and innovative processes. The team is motivated to generate ideas and proceed to achieve solutions that can be implemented. Thus proper attention may not be given to *discovery,* witnessing and recording of patentable products, processes, and software. In managing the team, co-leaders must follow a process to identify and document patentable material.

Sponsors should sign an agreement concerning the ownership and disposition of any and all patents generated during the project. The rights of the individual and/or team inventor(s) should be made very clear. Also, compensation, if any, to the inventor(s) should be clearly defined. The patent process should be explained to the team by the co-leaders at the start of the project. Certainly, the patent process must be approved by the sponsors' Patent Counsel.

A general framework is suggested as follows:

1. Assign team members a journal book to record their ideas and associated notes.
2. Journal entries should be in ink. No erasers are permitted. Mistakes and/or material to be omitted should be neatly crossed out with a single line, initialed, and dated.
3. Each entry in the journal is dated and signed by the author at the end of each entry.
4. At a regular interval, for example, biweekly, entries to the journals should be read by a fellow team member, signed as a witness, and acknowledged that the material is understood.

5. Journals should be kept confidential within the team.
6. Co-leaders should inform the Patent Counsel as promising ideas develop.

An example journal format is provided in Appendix F.4. This format can be used in a journal (paper) or computer. It is advised that if the electronic medium is used, then a hard copy be generated for the author and witness signatures.

Co-leaders need to be cautious with the patent process that it doesn't become a motivator for some team members and a demotivator for others. The team needs to experience the intellectual excitement of the patent process and carry this spirit forward in daily activities.

Creative Process

Co-leaders must at all times encourage a *free expression* environment in all creative sessions. At the same time, co-leaders must manage the process of generating ideas. A person other than a team member is used to facilitate creative sessions. Also, a person other than a team member acts as a recorder of the material generated during the creative sessions. The facilitator and recorder can be the same person depending on the situation.

Co-leaders are responsible to ensure that each team member has the opportunity to fully participate in a creative session. This requires close observations of the human dynamics active in a creative session.

Innovative Process

Co-leaders prepare the team members to make the mental switch from the creative to the innovative process. This is done fully recognizing that in reality the creative and innovative processes combine and form a *solution system*. Yet while in the innovative phase, team members must think in practical and business terms in order to move ideas forth for implementation.

Co-leaders need to encourage dissenting views about the value of ideas yet at the same time not create a situation where valuable ideas may be rejected because of feelings generated by egos rather than facts.

Celebration

Hard work to achieve goals without celebration creates a vacuum in human satisfaction. If left unattended, the team can become nothing more than a machine . . . work, work, work and eventually come to resent the project. Thus, co-leaders need to hold a team celebration when each milestone is achieved in the schedule. The type of celebration can range from having everyone cheer to holding a pizza party. The significance of the milestone dictates the type of celebration. Co-leaders should ask the team what type of celebration is needed.

Celebration provides a time to reflect on what has been achieved and what needs to be achieved. It is a period to recharge the mental batteries, to think about what went right and what needs to be done differently. Celebration can be a powerful catalyst for team enlightenment about their importance and what they have been able to accomplish.

Results

From the beginning of the project, expected results provide the impetus for direction relative to the problem/situation statement and objectives. Team members get involved with the excitement of generating ideas and conducting simulations or building prototypes. Unless the team is managed, results can miss the objectives.

Co-leaders need to keep team members focused on results but to do so without hampering the creative and innovative processes. This can be done simply by reminding the team about expected result at the beginning of a creative or innovative session and then reviewing the session's output relative to satisfying the expected result criteria. In other words: Are we going in the right direction? If not, what must be changed? Answers to these questions set both direction and boundary conditions for future creative and innovative sessions.

Team members must be made aware of the fact that results they deem satisfactory may not be acceptable to the sponsors. Results must satisfy the sponsors' requirements. Compromise is not an option. Co-leaders need to manage the team to avoid negotiating results that require the sponsors to accept a compromise.

LESSONS LEARNED

1. Sponsors must be careful to select co-leaders with not only technical but also business and leadership abilities. A strong technical background with weak business and leadership abilities increases co-leader failure.

2. Launching the team cannot be just another event. Sponsors must openly communicate what they want the team to achieve and the importance of the team. Sponsors need to support the importance statement with adequate resources for the team to perform its function.

3. Co-leaders need to take charge immediately of managing the project and team. They need to instill a definite sense of direction and responsibility.

4. Project management principles are used to operate the project. The best approach is separation of managing the project from managing the team. The reason resides in the fact that the team must generate ideas and provide innovative solutions. Generally, project management details must be transparent to the team so the creative and innovative processes are not stifled.

5. Co-leaders define a top level plan and Gantt Chart. The team then develops a more detailed plan and Gantt Chart. In this approach, the team has ownership.

6. The three variable boundary conditions of time, cost, and innovation are managed by the co-leaders to achieve balance with regard to project objectives of schedule, budget, and solutions. The team is kept appraised of the status from an information standpoint.

7. Co-leaders avoided problems with managing the project and team by using a checklist. Co-leaders improved the list by adding additional items as experience was gained.

8. Co-leaders found that by using small work packages with expected outputs, they were able to determine the status of

the project and then take actions, as needed, to keep it on schedule.

9. Open and honest communication both at meetings and informal settings enabled the team to achieve milestones and avoid problems becoming aggravated and thus, jeopardize meeting the objectives.

10. Keeping proper records of the creative and innovative processes enabled the team to recall ideas rapidly, support idea building, and avoid losing a range of potentially good ideas.

11. Co-leaders found the guidelines for handling morale issues and conflict to be very helpful. These guidelines enabled quick resolution of morale issues and conflicts.

12. Guidance on using a journal to record ideas for potential patent purposes, keeps team members focused on the value of ideas. The sponsors' recognition policy for patent material by team members and teams created a positive view toward the project and sponsor.

SUMMARY

1. Sponsors set the stage for the project by defining a clear vision and mission statements, objectives, and expectations. They provide an *end date* for the project.

2. Co-leaders for the team are appointed by the sponsors. Business and leadership traits are required as well as technical expertise.

3. Co-leaders define a top level plan and schedule. The team then defines a more detailed plan and schedule.

4. Co-leaders are responsible to manage the project as well as manage the team. In a general sense, project management is transparent to the team. Managing the team is vital to ensuring that the team is able to function effectively and efficiently in the creative and innovative processes.

5. Project management is directed to keep cost, time, and innovation in balance relative to budget, schedule, and solutions. Co-leaders are advised to keep the schedule on track from the beginning of the project and to take action(s) to correct problems immediately. The use of small work packages with identifiable and measurable output relative to expected output enables the co-leaders to determine project progress.

6. Team management insight and guidelines cover: a. keeping the team advised about the schedule, b. communication, c. morale issues, d. conflict resolution, e. benchmarking, f. patents, g. creative process, h. innovative process, i. celebration, and j. results.

7. Lessons learned from operating the customer-supplier innovation team are covered.

8. The reader is presented with a series of questions regarding the operation of the customer-supplier innovation team.

QUESTIONS

1. What is the process for operating the customer-supplier innovation team? How does it work?

2. What model is used?

3. What are the elements that comprise the process?

4. What measures, metrics, and measurements are used to determine operational status/acceptance?

5. Why does the operational process work for the team?

6. What hasn't worked in the operational process?

7. Why hasn't the operational process worked for the team?

8. What are some examples of successful customer-supplier innovation team operations?

9. Why were the examples successful?

10. What inputs are provided to the team by customers and suppliers?

11. What problems are experienced by the co-leaders?

12. How are these problems solved?

13. How does the team evaluate competition?

14. How often are meetings held among team members?

15. What is the relationship of the co-leaders? How do they resolve their differences?

16. How does the team and its members keep focused on what is required?

17. What operational lessons have been learned?

18. What changes should be made in view of greater operational experience?

19. What check list items should the co-leaders use in operating the team?

20. What approach to scheduling and reporting is used?

21. How is patent protection provided for customer-supplier, team, and team member?

Reward System and Refurbishment

"It is not the going out of port, but the coming in, that determines the success of a voyage."

Henry Ward Beecher

REWARD SYSTEM

Introduction

When sponsors launch a project, an important fact is communicated to the team. The team will be rewarded for successful accomplishment of the project. A simple statement! Everyone feels good. Yet, unless the reward system is carefully designed, the influence on the team's performance could be positive or negative. A reward system comprises positive reinforcement, recognition, and reward. Daily reinforcement of team members for positive behaviors can be recognized and rewarded based on the expected results these behaviors produce. Also, consideration must take into account any precedent that is established with the reward system and its influence on the operation of future teams.

Customer-supplier innovation teams are unique when it comes to the reward process. Unique because members come from two different cultures for example customer and supplier. In most companies, the culture shapes a reward system. Thus, the sponsors must work together to define a reward system that is best suited for the team in view of its expected results. The tendency may be to create a composite system from the sponsors' existing systems. This could be a big mistake depending on the *leading edge* extent of these systems. A better approach is to define a reward system and then determine to what extent, if any, the sponsors' reward system can satisfy the newly defined system. Sponsors assign individuals from human resources to design a reward system. These individuals are authorized to make the necessary decisions to define a reward system. Sponsors approve the reward system.

Customer and Supplier Culture

A Fortune 500 company's division approaches one of its first-tier suppliers about participating in a customer-supplier innovation team. The customer is from the automotive industry sector. The supplier's revenue is $250 million with 1500 employees. The supplier is considered a traditional manufacturer, a supplier willing to do what it takes to satisfy its customer.

The customer is progressive and considered a leading edge competitor within its industry. Two years ago, the customer received the Malcolm Baldrige National Quality Award. The customer uses project teams extensively. The CEO at the customer comes from a financial background. Backgrounds of the executive group range from marketing, manufacturing, and finance to political science. The executive staff spends a large percentage of its time addressing strategic issues.

The supplier wants to be progressive and looks to its customer for guidance. The supplier isn't familiar with project teams. The supplier is recognized as having very competent and professional people. The supplier does produce and manufacture cutting edge products. The supplier executives possess engineering backgrounds. The CEO of the supplier is an engineer and spends time involved with the engineering designs.

When we think about a company's culture, there is some confusion in reaching a common definition since many definitions exist because anthropologists, sociologists, psychologists, and quality professionals bring the views of their areas with them. Schein (1985) developed a model that seems to make sense out

Table 8.1. Cultural profile (example).

Cultural Profile Example			
	Behaviors	Values	Assumptions
Customer	1. Win 2. Teams 3. Business driven	1. Continuous improvement 2. End user satisfaction	1. Industry leader
Supplier	1. Follow customer 2. Engineering driven	1. Customer satisfaction	1. Obtain business 2. Keep business 3. Grow business

of the various views. The model suggests that there are three levels in representing a culture: 1. behaviors and artifacts, 2. beliefs and values, and 3. underlying assumptions. Schein arranged these levels according to observation. The underlying assumptions are the most difficult to observe. In fact, effort must be expended to determine their meaning. Perceiving, thinking, and evaluating the world, self, and others helps to uncover underlying assumptions.

So with a cultural model and the description of the customer and supplier, cultural profiles can be created. These profiles are essential in order to define a meaningful reward system based on reality as opposed to one structured on speculation. An example is shown in Table 8.1. The cultural differences shown in this example require acknowledgement and agreement by both parties as formulation of the rewards system occurs before the start of the project. One concern from the example is the fact that the supplier is not experienced in using project teams.

National and International Cultures

The total quality movement fueled by the Malcolm Baldrige National Quality Award suggests that excellent companies have strong corporate cultures. Further, there is a definite link between culture and performance. However, a corporate culture doesn't immediately translate to its subsidiaries. There is a difference in cultural environments. This becomes a focal point when integrating a corporate culture with the cultures of its national and international subsidiaries to achieve a unified and constant culture. Primarily, a corporate culture provides behavioral control for instilling the values that are expressed by employees as "this is the way we do things around here." Companies of excellence have achieved successful translation in this regard. For example, a customer doing business with Federal Express, from any geographic location, expects to find cultural consistency. This translates into a known delivery of performance.

When a company's culture must blend with another company for the formation of a customer-supplier innovation team, the approach used to instill a corporate culture with its subsidiaries can be equally applied. The key involves the customer and supplier identifying their respective cultures, analyzing the differences, and then creating a consistent composite culture for the team. The composite culture can then serve to guide the design of the reward system.

The process to arrive at the composite culture involves the steps shown in Figure 8.1. Obviously, this requires complete and open honesty on the part of customer and supplier. Hidden agendas and unwillingness to "tell all and tell it like it is" will not produce the intended understanding needed to define the composite culture.

Composite Culture and the Team

So far in this chapter, the reward system has been discussed and formulation made from the viewpoint of the customer and supplier relative to team members and the team. It is equally important that team members and the team viewpoints be presented. The success of the customer-supplier innovation team is related to the extent that belief, motivation, and achievement of expected results occur.

It's team members and the team that make things happen, not guidelines and standards. Besides, all the discussion about the design of the reward system and associated guidelines are

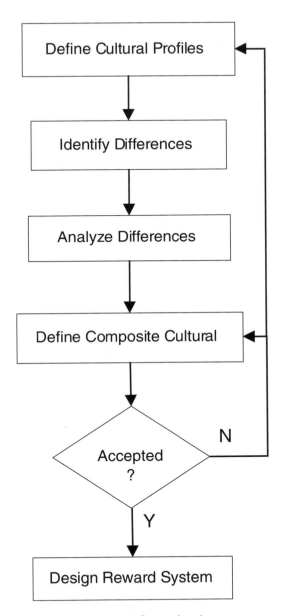

Figure 8.1.   Composite cultural flow chart.

directed to providing a set of values that enable team members and the team to perform at their full potential. Remember, make the plan, work the plan.

A critical element in the design of the reward system is obtaining input from team members. (Schuster 1984). What type of reinforcement, recognition, and reward are most important? Why is this so? When should it be administered?

The idealism and pragmatic development of a reward system will only be as good as the acceptance by team members. A compounding factor comes into view when the customer is sophisticated in outlook and practice and the supplier is responsive but lacks such sophistication. The team members from the supplier will be overwhelmed with the exposure to new thinking even though a composite culture is applied for team operation.

For example, the customer uses a team approach for all task and projects. The supplier uses a group approach where people in the group are experts in specific areas but do not have accountability for the outcome. Further, team members from the supplier are competitive on an individual basis with each other and do not share information readily. Team members from the customer are very sharing and comfortable with a team arrangement.

It is advisable that a viewpoint comparison chart be made from input received from the team members. An example is shown in Figure 8.2. This chart will provide the sponsors with *real* world input as they proceed to define the composite culture critical to formulation of the reward system. A worksheet to define the team viewpoints is provided in Appendix G.1.

Cultural Shaped Reward System

Sponsors can now proceed to discuss the design for the reward system. As stated previously in this chapter, the reward system comprises these processes: 1. reinforcement, 2. recognition, and 3. reward. Measures, metrics, and measurements are required to establish facts for these processes. Facts enable responsible administration of the reward system.

Reinforcement. Behaviors of team members and the team determine performance. These behaviors set the stage for success or

Team Members' Viewpoints
(Example)

	Customer	Supplier
Teams	Extensive	Limited
Idea Sharing	Open	Guarded
Reinforcement	Frequent positive comments	Frequent negative comments
Recognition	Public articles Formal dinners	T-shirts Pizza parties
Rewards	Cash Bonus Promotions Patents	Not consistent Not adequate Late administration Cash Bonus

Figure 8.2.   Team members' viewpoints (example).

failure of a task or project. Co-leaders can best manage behaviors of team members and the team by simply recognizing a basic behavioral principle: "behavior is a function of consequence." This principle resulted from the research work of behavioral psychologists and scientists such as Skinner (1969). A relationship model evolved, Figure 8.3. The model's meaning is straightforward. Activators cause a behavior to occur. Consequences determine whether a behavior will continue, decrease, or increase.

Positive reinforcement as a consequence improves behavior. For example, a team member contributes very enthusiastically during a brainstorming session. At the conclusion of the session, a co-leader compliments the team member for his contribution. The team member is pleased to hear the compliment. This compliment represents positive reinforcement. At the next brainstorming session, the team member generated ideas of even better quality than the previous session. Positive reinforcement creates a desirable consequence. As a result, the rate of response

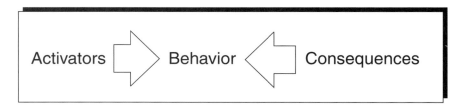

Figure 8.3. Behavior relationship model.

increases and behavior improves. Also, positive reinforcement can occur from a team member seeing the results of his or her work or approval from other team members.

Co-leaders need to use judgement in giving positive reinforcement. Positive reinforcement given to one team member may be negative to another team member. For example, all team members cannot be encouraged equally to take high risks on approaches to task assignments. Some team members would be slow to recover if a high-risk approach resulted in failure. Whereas other team members would take failure as a learning opportunity and charge ahead on a different approach.

The positive reinforcement process should be immediate when observable behavior occurs. This can be a simple *thank you* for a task well done or praise in front of other team members. When a task is completed, co-leaders must ensure that the results from the task are immediately evaluated and feedback given to team members. Co-leaders must always keep in mind that *behavior ignored will die.* For example, one or more team members that worked to complete a task and didn't receive feedback in a timely manner will be more inclined to not work as hard on the next task. Creating an environment of common courtesy and respect helps to perpetuate positive reinforcement.

Examples of measures, metrics, and measurements for exhibited behaviors are shown in Table 8.2. Measures could be taken for team member behavior involving confronting, mediating, dominating, and labeling. The sponsors must identify *targeted* behavior guidelines for co-leaders to follow. Co-leaders need to keep a record of their positive reinforcement efforts and the levels of achievement. This factual database is needed for applying the reward process.

Table 8.2.   Behavioral measurement (examples).

	Example 1	Example 2	Example 3
Measure	Can-do spirit	Sharing	Consensus support
Metric	Frequency	Frequency	Frequency
Measurement	Number of times required vs. number of times exhibited	Number of times required vs. number of times exhibited	Number of times required vs. number of times exhibited

Recognition. The team member and/or team complete a task that meets or exceeds expectations. This achievement calls for recognition. The sponsors must identify guidelines for the co-leaders to use. In all cases, recognition needs to be timely and not delayed so that the effectiveness of the recognition is not diminished or lost. For example, when a patent is filed, there needs to be recognition associated with the type and level for a patent process. Records of recognition activities should be kept by the co-leaders. These record will provide input to the reward process.

Rewards. The project is completed. The extent that expected results are achieved needs to be established. Sponsors must identify guidelines for the co-leaders to use. Co-leaders use the data and information from the reinforcement and recognition processes as input in determining the administration of the reward process.

A worksheet for sponsors to formulate reward system guidance for the co-leaders is provided in Appendix G.2.

Reward System Design

A guideline for designing a reward system is presented in Figure 8.4. A reward system design worksheet is provided in Appendix G.3.

An expansion of the points in Figure 8.4 is offered as follows:

Clean Sheet. Start without reference to any reward system or aspects of a system that may exist at one or both of the sponsors. A *clean sheet* mentality is needed to create the best reward system for the team.

Reward System Design Guidelines

1. Start with a *clean* sheet of paper
2. Make a clear statement for the purpose of the reward system
3. Determine the alignment of the reward system with: a. strategic results, b. tactical results, c. creative and innovative tasks, and d. critical behavior—member and team
4. Level, type, and timing of pay-out
5. Define measures, metrics, and measurements for reinforcement, recognition, and reward processes
6. Define the reinforcement, recognition, and reward processes
7. Keep the reward system simple
8. Compare the proposed reward system with existing reward systems used by sponsors. Revise proposed reward system, if necessary

Figure 8.4. Reward system design guidelines.

Reward System Purpose. Sponsors define the purpose. An example: "The purpose of the Customer-Supplier Innovation Team Reward System is to recognize the effort expended by the team to produce the expected results within the time, cost, and innovation boundary conditions."

Reward System Alignment.
Strategic Results. Sponsors must consider the impact of the team's results on the strategic business plan. If there is significant impact then this contribution needs to be included as a factor in determining the level of payout when the expected results are completely satisfied.

Tactical Results. Sponsors must consider if the impact of the team's results are limited to solely a tactical level.

Creative and Innovative Tasks. Sponsors must consider the contribution of the performance during the creative and innovative tasks. Also, any potential patents that were devised.

Targeted Behaviors. Sponsors need to define the targeted behaviors of the members and the team as related to producing expected results. For example: a *can-do* spirit would be essential for compressed time project.

Payout: Level, Type, and Timing. This can be very tricky since salary differences between customer-supplier team members could result in *equal* team members receiving different reward amounts. Sponsors need to be careful that this situation doesn't create negative behaviors. Depending on the project, sponsors need to determine where a cash, stock, or some other type of payout will be used. Whatever the level and type of payout, it must be given to the team members at the time an act is acknowledged and at the immediate closing of the project. Usually, this is done with some type of ceremony to honor the team members.

Reinforcement Process. Sponsors define the steps needed to reinforce positive behavior of team members.

Recognition Process. Sponsors define the steps to recognize achievements of members and the team during the operation of the project. Again this must be defined so that it represents a positive reinforcement of behavior and motivates the team.

Reward Process. Sponsors define the reward process to ensure the rewards are realistic and relate to the deliver of *expected results*.

Measures, Metrics, and Measurements. Sponsors define the measures, metrics, and measurements for the reinforcement, recognition, and reward processes.

Keep the Reward System Simple. Complexity of a reward system will act as a demotivator since such complexity may appear as though there are hidden elements that in the final analysis will detract from the payout. For example, a formula that takes factors into account that may not really have anything to do with the achievement of the expected result. The calculation could be based simply on the results achieved and everyone on the team receives the same payout. Sponsors must decide when expected results are not achieved, whether or not a partial payout is made. Caution is advised on this point since rewarding partial results may endorse mediocrity; for example, it is all right not to succeed. The reward system can be refined for future use with other project teams.

Proposed Reward System. The proposed reward system was developed from a *clean* sheet of paper approach. Aspects of existing reward systems at the sponsors were not considered initially. This approach is taken to remove any bias and to recognize the uniqueness of the customer-supplier innovation team. A comparison of existing reward systems with the proposed reward system can be made and, if necessary adjustments made. Most likely such adjustments will be very minor because of the team's uniqueness.

Reward System Operation

The best-designed reward system will be no better than the manner in how it is operated. Key operational factors to take into account are shown in Figure 8.5.

An elaboration of the points listed in Figure 8.5 are as follows:

1. **Team members value the system**—In designing the reward system, team members are given the opportunity to provide input. The approved reward system is endorsed by team members. Therefore, members value the reward system as a realistic method to enable them to achieve extra compensation or recognition for producing the expected project results.

2. **System is simple**—The system is straightforward in that the reward will be paid-out. It is a *go* or *no-go* method. The expected results are either achieved and the payout is made or there isn't a payout because the results were not achieved. The need for forms to be filled out and layers of management approval doesn't exist.

3. **Performance standard control**—The team controls whether they succeed or not. The performance standard recognizes a *go* or *no-go* acceptance of results. The

Reward System Operational Guidance

1. Team members value the system
2. System is simple to understand
3. Team can control performance standards
4. Co-leaders maintain the system
5. Open communication

Figure 8.5.   Reward system operation guidance.

objectives for the project are such that hard work on the part of the team will enable objectives to be achieved.

4. **Co-leaders maintain the system**—Co-leaders must be motivated to adequately manage the project and team to provide the highest probability that the team will be successful. This is accomplished by the sponsors providing the co-leaders with adequate base pay compensation. Also, co-leaders may be afforded a higher level of payout from the reward system when the expected results are achieved. Co-leaders are expected to reinforce positive behaviors of the team members on a daily basis.

5. **Open Communication**—Team members feel free to bring up problems that prevent achievement of the expected results and thus, payout from the reward system. The co-leaders must not allow the drive to achieve the payout from the reward system to be cause for demotivation of the team. For example, one or more team members is always pushing to move ahead at a minimum level for project milestones that will satisfy the expected project result at a minimum level while it is possible for the team to do even better than minimum achievement.

Types of Rewards

The type of rewards available can be applied to a team member and/or to the team. Sponsors must decide on the level of application. The types of reward are shown in Figure 8.6.

An explanation of the types of rewards is covered as follows:

1. **Member: Bonus**—This is a cash payout at the end of the project made only when expected results are achieved. It is calculated as a percentage of the base salary for the member. This can cause a problem because of the different salary levels of members and equality of team members. Also, members could be given in addition to the cash payout, a job promotion that includes a raise.

2. **Member: Profit sharing**—A percentage of the profits are paid depending on the return received from the implementation of the product, service, process, or system. It is paid after a set period of time has elapsed from the point of implementation. Financial data exist in order to make such a calculation. The frequency of the payment is determined by the sponsors and communicated before starting the project.

3. **Member: Gain sharing**—A percentage of the cost savings are paid depending on the return received from the implementation of the product, service, process, or system. It is paid after financial data exists to validate the savings. The frequency of the payment is determined by the sponsors and communicated before starting the project.

4. **Member: Cash**—A one-time cash payment can be made to the member. This type of cash payout is usually inflated to cover taxes so that the recipient nets the amount intended after taxes.

5. **Member: Patents**—A fixed cash payout is made at the time the patent is filed and again when the patent is granted. Depending on the arrangement of the member with the sponsors, royalties may also be included. The compensation associated with patents must be clearly understood before starting the project.

Types of Rewards

Level	Type
Member	Bonus
	Profit sharing
	Gain sharing
	Cash
	Patents
	Trip
	Stock options
	Promotion
Team	Bonus
	Profit sharing
	Gain sharing
	Cash
	Patents
	Trip
	Stock options

Figure 8.6. Types of rewards.

6. **Member: Trip**—An all-expenses paid trip for two people of a one or two weeks duration.

7. **Member: Stock Options**—Shares of stock are given to the member. The number of shares is a function of the level for the accomplishment and the price of the stock.

8. **Member: Promotion**—The demonstrated contribution of a team member can be rewarded with a promotion. This is a function of the level of the contribution and future career growth. In some cases, other rewards may also be given to a team member.

9. **Team: Bonus**—A cash payout is made only when expected results are achieved. It is calculated based on the expected value of the result. All members of the team receive the same amount of payout. The payout can be in the form of cash or company stock.

10. **Team: Profit Sharing**—A percentage of the profits are paid depending on the return received from the implementation of the product, service, process, or system. It is paid after a set period of time has elapsed from the point of implementation and financial data exist in order to make the calculation. The frequency of payment is determined by the sponsors and communicated before starting the project.

11. **Team: Gain Sharing**—A percentage of the cost savings are paid depending on the return received from the product, service, process, or system. It is paid after financial data exists to validate the savings. The frequency of the payment is determined by the sponsors and communicated before starting the project.

12. **Team: Cash**—A one-time cash payment can be made to the member. This type of cash payout is usually inflated to cover taxes so that the recipient nets the amount intended after taxes.

13. **Team: Patents**—There may be instances where more than one member is entitled to a patent. A fixed cash payout is made at the time the patent is filed and again when the patent is granted. Depending on the arrangement of the members with the sponsors, royalties may also be included.

The compensation associated with patents must be clearly understood before starting the project.

14. **Team: Trip**—An all expenses paid trip for two people of a one or two weeks duration.

15. **Team: Stock Options**—Shares of stock are given to the member. The number of shares is a function of the level for the accomplishment and the price of the stock.

Management of the project work environment and the behaviors of team members is directed to produce the expected results. As noted earlier, the reward system is comprised of three processes: reinforcement, recognition, and reward. The applications and methods associated with these processes are shown in Table 8.3.

Reward System Pros and Cons

The purpose of a reward system is to encourage positive behaviors on the part of team members and ultimately improve the team's performance to achieve expected project results. The idea of reward systems to influence behaviors is based on B. F. Skinner's behavior modification system. Yet, some reward systems have failed to produce expected results. Thus, reward systems have been criticized (Kohn 1993). The central reason for criticism resides with that fact that Kohn regards behavioral reward practices as manipulative and control-driven. He believes that team members need to experience satisfaction from the work itself rather than extrinsic satisfaction created by reward systems.

Skinner (1969) determined that behavior is a function of the external environment and controlling variables that allow observers to predict outcomes. The issue isn't whether positive or negative sources of control exist in the environment. These sources are observable. The real challenge is to understand how environmental variables affect behavior. Management of these variables will then produce positive behaviors with a corresponding impact on team members and consequently, team performance. Therefore, reward systems must incorporate effective behavior management relative to the work environment.

Table 8.3. Reward system management.

Reward System Management		
Processes	Applications	Methods
Reinforcement	Behavior	Coaching
Recognition	Project task	Handshake T-shirts Public article Celebration
Rewards	Results	Promotions Cash Bonus Profit sharing Gain sharing Patents Stock options

(Armitage 1997). Positive behavior of team members better ensures improved performance. Key points associated with the pros and cons for a reward system are presented in Figure 8.7.

REFURBISHMENT

Burnout Warning Signs

At the beginning of the project, team members are informed about the project's *end* date. It is very important to the morale of team members that they realize their project is for a finite time. The purpose is to avoid member *burn out*. Job *burn out* results from prolonged work stress. When recognized, the team member needs to receive treatment. However, a team member can help to prevent his or her burnout by exercising daily and following a process for proper nutrition.

Summary: Reward System Pros and Cons

Pros

1. Use team member
   input to formulate system
2. Managed work environment
3. Managed behaviors
4. Improved performance
5. System learning for
   continuous improvement

Cons

1. Requires work environment
   management
2. Requires competent co-leaders
3. Requires daily reinforcement
4. Demotivation from incentive
   inequities

Figure 8.7. Summary: Reward system pros and cons

All team members need to be aware of *burnout* warning signs. Everyone needs to look out for the other person. A guide for burnout warning signs is shown in Figure 8.8.

A brief description of the burnout warning signs are (Freudenbeger and Pichelson 1989) as follows:

1. **Exhaustion.** Lack of energy associated with feelings of tiredness and trouble keeping up with usual activities.

2. **Detachment.** Team member headed for burnout begins putting distance between themselves and fellow team members.

3. **Boredom and cynicism.** The burned-out team member begins to question the value of friendships and activities and even life itself.

4. **Increased impatience and irritability**—Burned-out team members usually have been able to do things quickly. However, as burnout takes hold, the team member's ability to do things diminishes and the team member becomes impatient and begins to blame fellow team members and others for things that are his/her own fault.

5. **Feelings of not being appreciated**—Burned-out team members want to be appreciated for their added efforts

---

Burnout Symptoms

1. Exhaustion
2. Detachment
3. Boredom and cynicism
4. Increased impatience and irritability
5. Feelings of not being appreciated
6. Change of work style
7. Paranoia
8. Disorientation
9. Psychosomatic complaints
10. Suicidal thinking

Figure 8.8. Burnout symptoms.

which aren't really producing more but less. These feelings result in the burned-out team member becoming bitter, angry, and resentful.

6. **Change of work style**—Reduced results and conflicts with other team members eventually causes a burned-out team member to withdraw from decisive leadership and work habits, or to compensate for conflicts by becoming more demanding, tyrannical, or inflexible.

7. **Paranoia**—Long-term burnout can lead a team member to believe that someone is out to get them.

8. **Disorientation**—Long-term burnout causes the team member's thoughts to wonder, speech pattern to falter and concentration spans to become limited. The team member may joke about becoming senile but inwardly, stress and agitation are the problem.

9. **Psychosomatic complaints**—Physical ailments such as headaches, lingering colds, backaches and similar complaints flourish in burned-out team members. Although the complaints may have real physical causes, they are more likely brought on by emotional stress, which the team member may or may not want to admit.

10. Suicidal thinking—As depression progresses, the results can lead to suicidal thinking.

Considerable information about burnout is available on the Internet. The reader is invited to use a search engine and job *burnout* as the key word to start surfing.

LESSONS LEARNED

1. Sponsors must secure input from team members to support formulation of a reward system.

2. Team members must be informed about the reward system at the time the project is launched.

3. Measures, metrics, and measurements must be defined by the sponsors for the reinforcement, recognition, and reward processes.

4. Co-leaders need to be educated and trained in the reinforcement, recognition, and reward processes.

5. When all is said and done, team members and their attitude toward the reward system will determine its success.

6. Recognizing that the customer and supplier cultures are different and defining a composite culture for the team supports more effective team operation.

7. Positive reinforcement must occur on a daily basis. This places considerable pressure on the co-leaders since they are the administrators of the positive reinforcement process.

8. The best operational situation occurs when team members remain focused on the work and the project objectives without undue attention and fanfare about the reward system.

9. Care must be exercised in order to have the reward system not act as a demotivator because of poor administration. When co-leaders determine that a problem exists, this problem needs to be resolved immediately.

10. When it becomes necessary to file patents, recognition should occur immediately. If the entire team is not credited for a patent filing since it is either for an individual team member or several team members, then care must be exercised to keep the situation positive and motivational.

11. The recognition system should not address base salaries of team members because of differences in salary scales between the customer and supplier.

SUMMARY

1. Sponsors design the reward system. Input is obtained from team members during the design process. Guidelines are provided for the design process.

2. Sponsors create a composite culture for the team operation. Also, the composite culture provides direction for formulation of the reward system.

3. The reward system is communicated to team members at the beginning of the project.

4. Co-leaders are responsible for administration of the reward system.

5. Sponsors are responsible for administration of a reward system for the co-leaders.

6. Positive reinforcement on a daily basis is essential to keep the team motivated.

7. Patent recognition and reward can be on a team member and/or team basis depending on the circumstances.

8. A reward system is effective when an understanding exists on how environmental variables affect behavior of team members and the team. Effective behavior management is necessary and the responsibility of the co-leaders.

9. Lessons learned regarding the reward system and refurbishment for the customer-supplier innovation team are presented.

10. Lessons learned regarding the reward system and refurbishment for the customer-supplier innovation team are presented.

11. The reader is presented with a series of questions concerning the reward systems and the refurbishment process applied to the customer-supplier innovation team.

QUESTIONS

1. When is the customer-supplier team told about the reward system?

2. What comprises the reward process?

3. How does the reward process work?

4. What are the criteria for being a recipient of the reinforcement, recognition, and reward processes?

5. What is the role of the co-leaders in the reward system?

6. Why is positive reinforcement important?

7. Who should receive reinforcement, recognition, and reward—individuals or team?

8. What are examples of reinforcement, recognition, and reward?

9. How is the reward system administered?

10. What is the acceptance of the customer-supplier innovation team regarding the reward system?

11. Is there a conflict between customer and supplier cultures that impacts the reward system?

12. What are the advantages/disadvantages of using a reward system?

13. When should the team be refurbished?

14. Why is it important to refurbish the team?

15. What is the refurbishment process?

16. What is burnout?

17. What steps can be taken to avoid burnout?

18. What is the role of co-leaders in observing and handling burnout situations?

19. What are the lessons learned about refurbishment?

Results

"Results? Why, man, I have gotten a lot of results. I know 50,000 things that won't work."

Thomas Edison

WHAT'S IT ALL ABOUT?

After all the rhetoric, results and only results are what really matters. Even the Malcolm Baldrige National Quality Award was changed to recognize the importance of results by assigning a scoring weight of 450 points out of 1000 to Category 7, Business Results. Without a doubt, the United States is heavily dependent on creative technology for innovation and productivity. Also, this applies to other developed countries. Competitive edge results are needed. A very active, continuous innovative process must be used to produce newer and better results for products, services, processes, and systems.

The customer-supplier innovation teams provide a solution for a more structured and better guarantee to achieve expected results within time, costs, and innovation boundary conditions. The model in Figure 9.1 provides a guide. By using this model, companies can understand and manage the cause and effect aspects of the customer-supplier innovation team. In other words, rather than the results occurring without fully understanding the reason, success is better assured with the model.

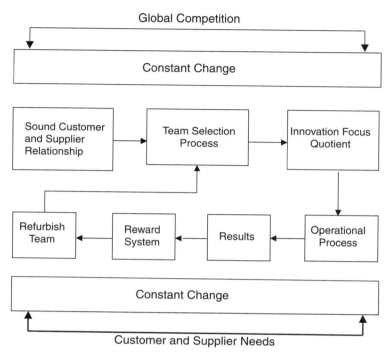

Figure 9.1. Customer-Supplier innovation team model.

Examples Abound

Customer-supplier innovation teams are quietly at work in small and large companies.

Results being achieved are significant. For example:

The 3M™ Trizact™ Abrasive products that are based on mircoreplication that advance the state-of-the art for consistent and more precise material removal (Norausky 1999).

General Motors Truck Group and the Behr innovation team used a unique magnetorheological fluid to advance the state-of-the-art for radiator fan clutches. (Baker, K.R. 1998)

Ames Rubber's (Wendal 1995) defect reduction from 30,000 parts per million (PPM) to 10 parts per million. This occurred based on a relationship with Xerox. Ames implemented the Xerox quality model. Ames kept improving and in 1993, received the Malcolm Baldrige Quality Award.

Allied Signal's (Minahan 1997) defect rate of parts and materials from 35,000 PPM to 1902 PPM on a companywide basis.

Trident Precision Manufacturing's (Baldrige 1996) technicians working at Xerox's Product Development Laboratory developed a 600 unique piece assembly ahead of schedule in seven months and 30 percent below cost estimates. Trident became a recipient of the 1996 Malcolm Baldrige Quality Award.

Hershey Foods working in a customer-supplier innovation team arrangement was able to eliminate paper labels and switch to *in-mold label* for plastic syrup bottles. (Norausky 1999D).

Additional examples are publicized regularly from a diverse range of industries. In fact, leading edge companies find such publicity as good advertising with regard to their competitiveness. And, of course, stock analysts notice the impact to the bottom line.

Innovation Teams

Over the past thirty years, innovation teams have been used very successfully. In just the past five years, there has been an increase in the use of customer-supplier innovation teams. This interest is attributed to greater emphasis on improving the supply chain. GLOMAXX, LLC (Norausky 1999E) is leading the way in creating, developing, and operating customer-supplier innovation teams. Insights gained from one hundred thirty-four teams give an excellent indication of why *expected results* were achieved.

Team Composition. Results produced by customer-supplier innovation teams involved an average team size of eight members. Usually, the customer members exceed the supplier members, for example on a team of eight: five were customers and three were suppliers.

Team Culture. A culture that focuses on results as important, since such results satisfy sponsor expectations, provides a *can-do* spirit. This spirit electrifies everything team members do. It creates a perpetual motion like momentum that helps to drive the team to success.

Team Reward System. Positive reinforcement, done openly and honestly, sets the stage for motivation toward project results. Certainly, monetary compensation represents a tangible recognition and reward for members and team achievement. With a more transitory workforce and downsizing of companies, pay for achievement represents a realistic motivator. Caution is advised that pay for achievement is made only when *expected results* are realized. This requires measures and metrics that sponsors and team members agree to prior to starting a project. This enables a go, no-go decision relative to results and any subsequent payout. The value of patents and the contribution to protecting the *expected results* must not be overlooked.

Team Creativity. Creative ideas with the methods and techniques can be numerous. The key to channeling worthwhile ideas that ultimately lead to innovative ideas that are implemented as solutions for *expected results,* is a function of managing the process and the team. The team needs to be reminded during a free form creative idea generating process that a direction does exist. The technique involves timing of when and how the team is reminded while not diverting the team's creative energy from free form idea generation.

Team Innovation. The innovative process is a more openly directed effort toward solutions that can be implemented. The team must focus on *expected results* as the end product of their effort. Co-leaders manage the innovative process to achieve this objective. Results were remarkable when teams stayed focused and realized that their efforts were important and could make the difference. A strong sense of team belonging existed and when the project was completed, the team celebrated the project's success.

Managing the Project. Project management techniques are well known. The understanding and skill needed to apply these techniques truly does shape the outcome of the results. Strong and competent co-leaders produce results. Usually, these results satisfy or exceed sponsor requirements.

Managing the Team. Working with people is always a challenge but can be effectively and successfully managed when competent leadership is applied. Results come from the team. A strong team spirit with the proper focus produces *expected results.*

Refurbishment. The team has worked hard to deliver the *expected results.* Sponsors must keep their promise to disband the team once the project is completed. Team members need a mental and physical change. By keeping their promise, the sponsors establish creditability with future teams.

Also, co-leaders and team members by being vigilant were able to prevent burnout during the operation of the team.

By Industry Sector. High and medium-range technology sectors are using the customer-supplier innovation teams. Results in these companies are very encouraging and contribute to a strong competitive presence in their respective markets. Use in traditional industries is very slight. This is due in part because of the apparent lack of sophistication in traditional industries. Such industries are lean in both their thinking and resources. These industries will continue to experience shrinking margins and market loss and the majority will merge or be acquired by larger more sophisticated companies.

FUTURE FOR CUSTOMER-SUPPLIER INNOVATION TEAMS

Once Begun

An avalanche begins with a small movement of snow until an entire region becomes unstable and the avalanche proceeds down the mountainside. The use of customer-supplier innovation teams is a well kept secret of many companies. It isn't publicized and talked about as *customer-supplier innovation teams.* It is cloaked in terms like partnering, alliances, system engineering, and supply chain relationship. However, global competition is rooting out the true character of what constitutes successful competitive approaches. Customer-supplier innovation teams are being described. Like the avalanche, customer-supplier innovation teams are rumbling through organizations as a key competitive advantage. Interest is building on the part of non-adaptive companies. These companies are beginning to see the advantage of such teams. In fact, there isn't much choice. Once a critical number of customers, in leadership roles, use customer-supplier innovation teams to remain competitive, other companies have no choice but to follow.

Map for Success

The results from customer-supplier innovation teams were achieved by following a map for success. The process begins with a correct match between the sponsors, then progresses to team member selection and appointment, establishing the Innovation Focus Quotient, co-leaders designated and ensuring adequate resources are available. This is a people part of the map. The remainder involves the creative and innovative processes superimposed with the reward system and then managing the team and project. When viewed from a distance, the map for success simply involves managing people and processes. The secret for success is identifying and handling the details. The skill is doing it!

Future

The future for the customer-supplier innovation teams falls into four areas: 1. Shorten the time to get the team ready, 2. Define a process to increase the number of creative ideas that advance to the innovative process stage, 3. Reduce the time for prototyping and simulation, 4. Develop a culture where internal customer-supplier innovation teams can be set-up and operated rapidly following the map for success. The competitive playing field is being leveled with the rapid access to data and information. It is the customer and supplier that get to the market place the fastest to satisfy customers who become the winners.

Of future concern, especially with the impact of downsizing, is the shortened attention span and dedication of the people remaining in the work force. These people will need to become more adaptable to working in *true* teaming arrangements. As this is achieved and when the processes are applied correctly, then *expected results* will follow.

 ## LESSONS LEARNED

1. Excellent results today become normal after two to three years or sooner depending on whether the industry involves high technology or traditional manufacturing.

2. Setting high-expected results as objectives can be achieved with the right team, co-leaders, and adequate resources.

3. Team satisfaction becomes more important than project results when a clear business strategy isn't evident to team members.

4. The customer-supplier innovation team model offers processes to achieve results to meet sponsors' expectations provided the processes are followed.

5. Customer-supplier innovation teams represent an investment that warrants a proper return by achieving the expected results. These teams should be used for significant projects.

6. Managing both the team and project is necessary to achieve expected results.

7. Team members need to believe in the project to bring their full creativity to bear and produce expected results.

SUMMARY

1. The customer-supplier innovation team model defines adequate processes to produce expected results.

2. Customer-supplier innovation teams operate in small to large companies.

3. The use of innovation teams has increased over the past thirty years. Of particular interest is the increase in customer-supplier innovation teams. There has been a substantial increase in the past five years.

4. Sponsors committed support, co-leaders management of the project, team and processes produce expected results with customer-supplier innovation teams.

5. Staying competitive means being able to implement innovative solutions. This is a continuous process. After all is said and done, only timely innovative results make the difference for industry leadership.

6. Lessons learned regarding results achieved with the customer-supplier innovation team are covered.

7. The reader is presented with a series of questions concerning the process for achieving results with the customer-supplier innovation team.

QUESTIONS

1. What results have been produced with customer-supplier innovation teams?

2. Why are results produced by the customer-supplier innovation teams significant? Different?

3. How were these results achieved (measured)?

4. What do world-class companies do with customer-supplier innovation teams relative to results?

5. What process keeps customer-supplier innovation teams focused on required results?

6. Why does the process work to keep customer-supplier innovation teams focused?

7. What are expectations for future customer-supplier innovation team results?

APPENDICES

Appendix A.1.   Customer-Supplier relationship inventory worksheet.

Appendix B.1.   Needs table worksheet.

Appendix B.2.   Customer and Supplier relationship worksheet.

Appendix C.1.   Team charter worksheet.

Appendix C.2.   Team charter worksheet (example).

Appendix C.3.   Candidate selection worksheet.

Appendix D.1.   Personal creativity journal form.

Appendix D.2.   Creative ideas recording worksheet.

Appendix D.3.   Brainstorming worksheet.

Appendix D.4.   Brainstorming worksheet (example).

Appendix D.5.   Force field analysis worksheet.

Appendix D.6.   Force field analysis worksheet (example).

Appendix D.7.   Mind mapping worksheet.

Appendix D.8.   Mind mapping worksheet (example).

Appendix D.9.   Free association worksheet.

Appendix D.10.   Free association worksheet (example).

Appendix D.11.   Problem/Situation review worksheet—creative process.

Appendix E.1.   Problem/Situation review worksheet—innovative process.

Appendix E.2.   Problem/Situation review worksheet—innovative process (example).

Appendix E.3.   Idea elaboration worksheet.

Appendix E.4.   Dry run critique sheet.

Appendix F.1.   Sponsors project definition worksheet.

Appendix F.2.   Sponsors project definition worksheet— (example).

Appendix F.3.   Managing the project checklist.

Appendix F.4.   Patent journal format.

Appendix G.1.   Team viewpoints worksheet.

Appendix G.2.   Co-leader reward system worksheet.

Appendix G.3.   Reward system design worksheet.

Appendix A.1. Customer-Supplier relationship inventory worksheet.

Organization: **Prepared by:** **Date:**

Source	Vendor	Traditional Supplier	Certified	Partnership	Alliance	Potential C-S Innovation Team	Comments

Reference: completed Table 1.1 in Chapter 1.

Appendix B.1.   Needs table worksheet.

Date: **Location:**

Customer   **or**   **Supplier**   (Circle one)

Participants:

Recorder:

Need	Action
Price	
Quality	
Delivery	
Improvement	
Future Business	
Certification	
Incoming Inspection	
Shared Risk	
Financial Support	
Other	

Reference: completed Table 2.1 in Chapter 2.

Appendix B.2. Customer and Supplier relationship worksheet.

	Score	
	Customer	Supplier

Trust (300)
   Keeps promises (150)
   Education and Training (50)
   Incoming Inspection Eliminated (50)
   Certification (50)
	NA	NA

Communication (200)
   Communication lines all levels (50)
   Issues addressed and negotiated up-front (50)
   Responses to requests (50)
   Action to meet requirements (50)		

Commitment (200)
   Customer long term business (50)
   Supplier cost effective production (50)
   Make each other successful (50)
   Continuous improvement (50)
	NA	NA

Strategic Planning (100)
   Joint planning session (50)
   Operational plans (25)
   Items to meet strategic objectives (25)		

Prevention (100)
   Supplier preventive actions (40)
   Customer specification (40)
   Lessons learned (20)
	NA	NA

Cooperation (100)
   Identify and handle risks (50)
   Willingness to make each other successful (50)		

Total: _____

Appendix C.1.   Team charter worksheet.

Date: **Location:**

Charter Creators:
Customer: **Supplier:**

1. **Problem/Situation**

2. **Statement of Work**

3. **Number of Team Members**

   Customer: _____   Supplier: _____

Continued

Appendix C.1. *Continued.*

4. **Team Member Knowledge and Skill** (Complete for each required team member)

   From: Customer Team ☐ **or Supplier Team** ☐ (Check one)

   Knowledge (specify)

   • Technical—

   • Business—

   • Product—

   • Service—

   • Process—

   • System—

   • Other—

   Skill

   • Interpersonal—

   • Communication—

   • Other—

5. Resources

- Budget—

- Facilities (for example, office, shop, laboratory)—

- Equipment (for example, computers)—

- People (for example, support personnel)—

- Transportation (for example, vehicles)—

- Other—

6. Operational Guidelines

- Communication—

- Reward System—

- Conflict Resolution—

- Patents—

- Records—

- Other—

Continued

Appendix C.1. *Continued.*

7. Co-Leader Responsibility and Authority

8. Expected Results

9. Project Completion Date: _____

10. Agreed By:

_____		_____
Customer/Date		Supplier/Date

_____		_____
Title/Company		Title/Company

Appendix C.2.   Team charter worksheet (example).

Date: *January 12, 20xx*   **Location:** *Springfield, MA*

Charter Creators:
Customer: *Sam Tips, Bill Hugh*   **Supplier:** *Sandra Hills, Jim Goodson*

1. **Problem/Situation**

   Optical properties of glass are distorted by impurities found in silica.

2. **Statement of Work**
   - *Project is competitor sensitive. Team members are not to discuss with unauthorized personnel.*

   - *Determine a process to make pure silica.*

   - *Process must be capable of mass production.*

   - *Process must be cost effective.*

3. **Number of Team Members**
   Customer: ____4____   Supplier: ____3____

Continued

Appendix C.2. *Continued.*

4. **Team Member Knowledge and Skill** (Complete for each required team member). *[Example shown is for one team member.]*

From: Customer Team ☒ **or Supplier Team** ☐ (Check one)

Knowledge (specify)

- Technical—*Physical Chemistry (Ph.D.) Practical experience with research, development and production of optical glass.*

- Business—*Economics.*

- Product—*Twenty years experience with optical glass.*

- Service—*Not applicable.*

- Process—*Glass production processes. Leading edge knowledge.*

- System—*Integration of processes for specific glass systems.*

- Other—*Computer science. Hyperequations.*

Skill

- Interpersonal—*Good listener. Empathic. Values other people's views.*

- Communication—*Good written and oral presentations.*

- Other—*Building prototype glass process.*

5. Resources

- Budget—*$20 million per year.*

- Facilities (for example, office, shop, laboratory)—*10 person office with 3 conference rooms. Full office furniture. 20,000 ft² laboratory/prototype* line.

- Equipment (for example, computers)—*Cray 900-16 super computer link. Desk top 500MH$_z$ computers, color printers, cell phones with scramblers.*

- People (for example, support personnel)—*1 secretary, 1 facilitator, X technical experts are required.*

- Transportation (for example, vehicles)—*Private vehicle for each team member.*

- Other—

6. Operational Guidelines

- Communication—*Weekly e-mail reports to sponsors. Face-to-face monthly reports to sponsors. Team meeting weekly.*

- Reward System—*Sponsors defined and available.*

- Conflict Resolution—*Co-leader responsible to mediate resolution.*

- Patents—*Team members keep record books. Team members and co-leaders work with sponsors' legal council.*

- Records—*Records of all creative and innovative sessions.*

- Other—*Defined as project progresses.*

Continued

Appendix C.2.   *Continued.*

7. Co-Leader Responsibility and Authority
- Co-leaders are responsible to keep the project on schedule, under or on budget and deliver the expected results.

- Report directly to Presidents of sponsors.

- Full authority to take any and all actions as stated in this charter to achieve the expected results.

8. Expected Results
- Pilot process to make pure silica.

- Production process would be cost effective.

9. Project Completion Date: *May 31, 20xx*

10. Agreed By:

_____   _____
Customer/Date   Supplier/Date

President   Bacor Glass   *President Advance Materials*
Title/Company   Title/Company

Appendix C.3. Candidate selection worksheet.

Date: **Location:**

Candidate Name:

Evaluators: **Customer:**
                    Supplier:

Selection Criteria
(Record key comments made by the candidate. Score each criterion).

ITEM   SCORE

1. Interest (100 points)
[Candidate must be interested in and excited about the project. Why is the candidate interested and why does he/she believe they can make a contribution?]

2. Competency (100 points)
[Candidate's work success record should be outstanding. Candidate should describe how a complex problem/ situation was encountered and resolved. What innovative solutions were provided? How is he/she staying current in their field.]

3. Interpersonal Skills (100 points)
[Candidate needs to explain why he/she possess good inter-personal skills. Describe a situation where conflict was involved and the approach taken to obtain resolution.]

4. Communication (100 points)
[Candidate must be able to engage in effective conversations as well as presentations. Describe one-on-one conversation style. Provide evidence of effective presentations. Evaluate candidate's written reports for writing skill & competency of thought.]

Continued

Appendix C.3. *Continued.*

ITEM   SCORE

5. Curiosity (200 points)
[Candidate must exhibit a very high level of curiosity.
Candidate should give examples that demonstrate his/
her curiosity and the results of this curiosity.]

6. Change Practitioner (100 points)
[Candidate possesses a record of engaging the change
process successfully. Establish the extent a candidate is
a "risk taker." Candidate should explain process used to
engage people and organizations in the change process.]

7. System and Process Thinker (100 points)
[Candidate must provide evidence of thinking in systems
and process terms. Discuss examples of system and
process thinking and the results produced.]

8. Passion to Succeed (200 points)
[Candidate must exhibit evidence of passion to succeed
as both and individual and team member. Explain why
and how he/she would operate to ensure success as
individual and team member.]

- Individual

- Team Member

Total Score: _____

Appendix D.1.   Personal creativity journal form.

Date: Location:

Creative Idea:

Under what circumstances did I get the idea? How I felt at the time:
Happy/Neutral/Sad.

What am I going to do with the idea?

When?

Who else do I need to contact?

Comments:

Appendix D.2.   Creative ideas recording worksheet.

Date: **Location:**

Problem Statement/Situation:

Participants:

Recorder:

Idea Name/Number:

Statement of Idea(s):

Selection of Idea (State Basic Reason(s) Selected/Not Selected):

Look Back (If done) (State Basic Reason(s) Selected/Not Selected):

Appendix D.3. Brainstorming worksheet.

Date: **Location:**

Problem Statement/Situation:

Participants:

Recorder:

State Idea(s):

Appendix D.4.   Brainstorming worksheet (example).

Date: *January 20, 20xx*   **Location:** *Beachside Conference Room*

Problem Statement/Situation: *Motorcycle engine oil leakage*

Participants: *Jim Song, Patrick Kelly, Bill King, Sam Cummings, Joe Hu, Jill Sampson, Ben Murphy, Bob Ruse*

Recorder: *Jason Scribe*

State Idea(s):

- *Better gaskets*
- *Put a pan under the engine*
- *Eliminate gaskets*
- *Use rubber gaskets*
- *Replace the engine*
- *Put sealant on the gaskets*
- *Better mating surface for the gasket*
- *Use oil that doesn't leak*
- *Use fine threads for the bolts that secure the gaskets*
- *Reduce the number of surfaces that need gaskets*
- *Encapsulate the engine when not running*
- *Eliminate the need for oil*
- *Use a solid lubricant*
- *Design a new engine*
- *Make the engine a one piece item so gaskets aren't needed*
- *Increase the number of fasteners to clamp gaskets*
- *Weld the engine shut*
- *Use interlocking covers*
- *Change gasket material from cork to a liquid sealant*
- *Use mating parts that expand and contract together with thermal fluctuations*
- *Make engine parts that contain their own lifetime part lubricant*
- *Use a self tightening fasteners that compensate for thermal fluctuations*
- *Use a computer sensing gasket that indicates when a leak at a gasket location is eminent*

Appendix D.5.   Force field analysis worksheet.

Date: **Location:**

Problem Statement/Situation:

Participants:

Recorder:

I. Driving Forces (+)	Inhibiting Forces (−)

II. Significant Driving Force:

III. Significant Inhibiting Force:

IV. Changes to Problem Statement/Situation based on review of forces:

Continued

Appendix D.5. *Continued.*

V. Brainstorm ideas based on Problem Statement/Situation in Item IV:

VI. Evaluate ideas for input to innovative process:

Idea	Reason for Selection/Non-Selection

Appendix D.6. Force field analysis worksheet (example).

Date: *January 20, 20xx*   **Location:** *Cliffside Conference Room*

Problem Statement/Situation: *Market Share Declining*

Participants: *Sue Ping, Patrick Ballki, Larry Cladski, Bill Home, Leon Chu, Roger Brown, Malcolm Jenkins, Chris James*

Recorder: *Randy White*

I. Driving Forces (+)	Inhibiting Forces (−)
• *Capitalization* • *Excellent Facilities* • *Competent Workforce* • *Declining Stock Price* • *Strong Product Identity*	• *Global Competition* • *Newer Technology* • *Poor Quality* • *Late Deliveries* • *Poor Reliability*

II. Significant Driving Force:

Declining Stock Price
Capitalization

III. Significant Inhibiting Force:

Global Competition
Newer Technology

IV. Changes to Problem Statement/Situation based on review of forces:

Market share declining. (No change)

V. Brainstorm ideas based on Problem Statement/Situation in Item IV:

• *Re-engineer management*
• *Acquire newer technology*

Continued

Appendix D.6. *Continued.*

- *Install process control across enterprise*
- *Understand customer requirements*
- *Improve product reliability*
- *Introduce new publicity campaign base on strong product identity*
- *Reduce process cycle times*
- *Educate and train workforce on their responsibilities*
- *Presentation to Wall Street analysts on the re-defined company*
- *Understand the competition*

VI. Evaluate ideas for input to innovative process:

Idea	Reason for Selection/ Non Selection
• *Re-engineer management* • *Install process control across the enterprise* • *Reduce process cycle times* • *Acquire new technologies* • *Educate and train the workforce on their responsibilities*	**_Selected_** *Primary. Address the root causes.*
• *Understand customer requirements* • *Improve product reliability* • *Ensure workforce skills match technology requirements* • *Introduce new publicity campaign based on strong product identity* • *Reduce process cycle times* • *Educate and train the workforce on their responsibilities* • *Presentation to Wall Street analysts on the re-defined company* • *Understand the competition*	**_Not Selected_** *Secondary and tertiary level ideas relative to problem.*

Appendix D.7.   Mind mapping worksheet.

Date: **Location:**

Topic (Problem, Situation, Object, Concept) **Statement:**

Participants:

Recorder:

I.   **Mind Map** (See Figure A.1.):

II.   **Group Ideas from Mind Map I:**

     a. Common concepts

     b. Themes

III. **Ideas from Grouping in II:**

IV. **Ideas Selected/Not Selected:**

Figure A.1. Mind map form.

Appendix D.8.   Mind mapping worksheet (example).

Date: **Location:**

Topic (Problem, Situation, Object, Concept) **Statement:**

Participants:

Recorder:

I.   **Mind Map** (See Figure B.1.):

II. **Group Ideas from Mind Map I:**

   a. Common concepts
   Design   Specification
   Manufacturing   Material
   Equipment   Suppliers
   People

   b. Themes
   Lack of Control (Internal & External)
   Systems Breakdown
   Sense of business purpose not apparent

III. **Ideas from Grouping in II:**

   Educate and train all employees and suppliers.
   Define a comprehensive quality assurance system.
   Define an operational plan with measures, metrics, and measurements.

IV. **Ideas Selected/Not Selected:**

   Educate and train all employees and suppliers concerning their role in a quality system.
   Define a supplier certification program.

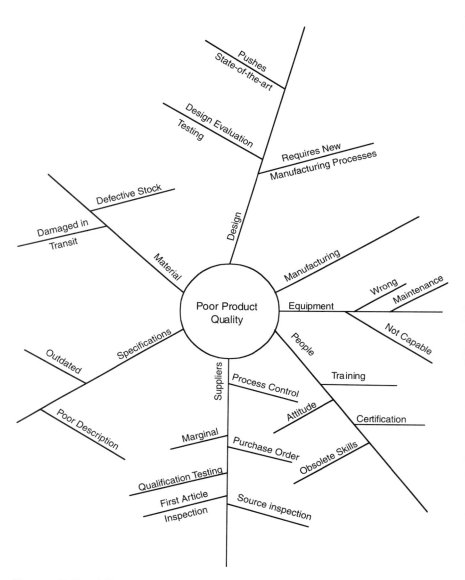

Figure B.1.   Mind map form example.

Appendix D.9.   Free association worksheet.

Date: **Location:**

Topic (Problem, Situation, Object, Concept) **Statement:**

Participants:

Recorder:

List of Thoughts	Brainstorm Ideas from Thoughts
1.	I.1.
2.	I.2.
3.	I.3.
4.	I.4.
5.	I.5.
6.	I.6.
7.	I.7.
8.	I.8.
9.	I.9.
10.	I.10.
11.	
12.	
13.	
14.	
15.	
16.	
17.	
18.	
19.	
20.	

Appendix D.10. Free association worksheet (example).

Date: *February 15, 20xx*   **Location:** *Mountain Side Conf. Rm.*

Topic (Problem, Situation, Object, Concept) **Statement:** *Ninety-five percent of parts are delivered late.*

Participants: *Jim Song, Patrick Kelly, Bill King, Sam Cummings, Joe Hu, Jill Sampson, Ben Murphy, Bob Ruse.*

Recorder: *Jason Scribe*

List of Thoughts	Brainstorm Ideas from Thoughts
1. *Late*	I.1. *Change manufacturing process*
2. *Faster*	I.2. *Modify delivery routing*
3. *Eliminate*	I.3. *Re-locate distribution centers*
4. *Schedule*	I.4. *Let customers do the pick-up*
5. *Time*	I.5. *Improve date of delivery quotes*
6. *Cycle*	I.6. *Sales and manufacturing communication*
7. *Repeat*	I.7. *Customer notification process*
8. *Pick-up*	I.8. *Reduce order entry cycle time*
9. *Convenient*	I.9. *Shorten order to delivery cycle time*
10. *Easy*	I.10. *Speed-up delivery process*
11. *Early*	
12. *On-time*	
13. *Ready*	
14. *Take*	
15. *Remove*	
16. *Change*	
17. *Shape*	
18. *Alter*	
19. *Improve*	
20. *Process*	

Appendix D.11.   Problem/Situation review worksheet-creative process.

Date: **Location:**

Participants:

Recorder:

1. **Problem/Situation Statement** (provided by sponsors):

2. **Root cause(s) for problem/situation:**

3. **Consequences of not having a solution:**

4. **Criteria solution must satisfy:**
5. **Change(s) to the problem/situation statement:**

   Change   Reason   Advantage

6. **Team consensus on required change(s) and agreement by sponsors:**

7. **Problem/situation Statement** (creative process). [Repeat if the same statement provided by the sponsors.]

Appendix E.1.   Problem/Situation review worksheet-innovative
process.

Date: **Location:**

Participants:

Recorder:

1. **Problem/Situation Statement** (used for creative process):

2. **Circumstances that impact the problem/situation
   statement:**
   a.

   b.

   c.

3. **Change(s) to the problem/situation statement:**
   Change   Reason   Advantage

4. **Team consensus on required change(s):**

5. **Problem/Situation Statement** (innovative process). [Repeat
   if the same statement used for the creative process.]

Appendix E.2. Problem/Situation review worksheet-innovative process.

Date: *March 15, 20xx*   **Location:** *White Water Lodge*

Participants: *Bill Wake, Sue High, Ben Jack, Hal Kowalski, Jim Norris, Frank Simmons*

Recorder: *Jack Swim*

1. **Problem/Situation Statement** (used for creative process):
   Rotor blade vibration occurs on all helicopter models.

2. **Circumstances that impact the problem/situation statement:**
   a. *Preliminary investigation revealed that rotor vibration only occurs on CD5 Helicopters.*
   b.

   c.

3. **Change(s) to the problem/situation statement:**

Change	Reason	Advantage
Only on CD5 Helicopters	*Vibration not on all helicopters*	*Focus on actual problem*

4. **Team consensus on required change(s):**
   Team agreed by consensus that the problem statement required a change to address the fact that rotor vibration only occurs on the CD5 Helicopter.

5. **Problem/Situation Statement** (innovative process). [Repeat if the same statement used for the creative process.]

   Rotor blade vibration is occurring on the CD5 Helicopter.

Appendix E.3.   Idea elaboration worksheet.

Date: **Location:**

Idea Name/Description:

Evaluators:

Recorder:

Strengths:

Weaknesses:

Additional data and information needs:

Disposition:

Responsible Team Member:

Appendix E.4.   Dry run critique sheet.

Title:

Presenter's Name: **Length of Time:**

- **Introduction**
  Opening Statement Captures Attention [ ] Yes [ ] No
  Comment _____

  Put the audience at ease. [ ] Yes [ ] No Comments _____

- **Slides**
  Content is easy to read. [ ] Yes [ ] No Comments _____

  Clarity (Can be understood.) [ ] Yes [ ] No Comments _____

  Slides are effective. [ ] Yes [ ] No Comments _____

  Other _____

- **Message of presentation**
  What is it? _____

  Clear? [ ] Yes [ ] No Comments_____

- **Presentation Style**
  Eye contact with the audience. [ ] Yes [ ] No
  Comments _____

  Voice projection, pitch, tone, and volume were satisfactory.
  [ ] Yes [ ] No
  Comments _____

  Reads Speech. [ ] Yes [ ] No Comments _____

  Reads Slides. [ ] Yes [ ] No Comments _____

  Body Language expressed confidence and enhanced presentation.
  [ ] Yes [ ] No
  Comments _____

  Gestures were not distracting. [ ] Yes [ ] No Comments _____

  Tempo of presentation was satisfactory. [ ] Yes [ ] No
  Comments _____

Continued

Appendix E.4.   *Continued.*

Showed sincere enthusiasm. [ ] Yes [ ] No Comments _____

Made logical, smooth transition between topics. [ ] Yes [ ] No
Comments _____

Handles Questions in an professional and knowledgeable manner.
[ ] Yes [ ] No
Comments _____

Use of humor was effective. Jokes and stories illustrated key
points. [ ] Yes [ ] No [ ] NA Comments _____

Provided a comprehensive, easy to follow summary. [ ] Yes [ ] No
Comments _____

- **Exit Transition**
  Introduces the next speaker/segment. [ ] Yes [ ] No
  Comments _____

- **Other Comments**

Appendix F.1.   Sponsors project definition worksheet.

Date: **Location:**

Sponsors: **Customer:**
                   Supplier:

Participants: **Customer:**
                   Supplier:
                   Team:

Recorder:

Vision:

Mission:

Objectives:

Expectations:

Project *End Date:*

Appointment of Team Co-Leaders:
   Customer: Supplier:

Problem/Situation Statement:

Preliminary Resources:

Appendix F.2. Sponsors project definition worksheet (example).

Date: *February 15, 20xx*   **Location:** *Running Spring Resort*

Sponsors: **Customer:** *Sonic Manufacturing*
                   Supplier: *Advanced Structures*

Participants: **Customer:** *Ron Jacobs, Sam Jennings*
                  Supplier: *Bill Sampson, Todd Clancy*
                  Team: *Sam Hogan, Bill Joneson, Patrick Harris,
                  Kim Kutton, Mary Smithson, Jacob Lamb,
                  Rene Cuba*

Recorder: *Jack Swain*

Vision: *Be recognized as the world-class manufacturer of super-sonic jet aircraft for business and private use.*

Mission: *Provide state-of-the-art supersonic jet aircraft to businesses.*

Objectives: *Provide a fuselage design that weights 30 percent less and 200 percent stronger.*

Expectations: *Objectives are cost-effective and provide leading edge solutions.*

Project *End Date:* *August 31, 20xx, 6 months after start of project.*

Appointment of Team Co-Leaders:
   Customer: *Bill Joneson*   Supplier: *Kim Kutton*

Problem/Situation Statement: *Current fuselage weight contributes to fuel consumption. Competitor aircraft are lighter in weight with improved fuel consumption. Engine design is similar.*

Preliminary Resources: *1) 5000 ft² office at a separate location from customer and supplier, 2) computer aided design equipment, 3) personal computers, 4) $2 million budget.*

Appendix F.3.   Managing the project check list.

1. **Schedule**
   ☐ Gantt Chart created
   ☐ Milestones reviewed
   Schedule: ☐ Behind, ☐ On ☐ Ahead
   ☐ Corrective actions: ☐ Assigned ☐ Not assigned, ☐ Completion date
   assigned
   ☐ Discussion with sponsors on end date. (☐ Meet ☐ Not met)
   ☐ Weekly report available: ☐ Yes ☐ No ☐ Action

2. **Budget**
   ☐ All team members aware of the budget.
   ☐ Budget review: ☐ Under, ☐ Over, ☐ On-target
   ☐ Action needed: When _____, Who _____
   Expected results and date _____
   ☐ Weekly report available: ☐ Yes, ☐ No, ☐ Action

3. **Solutions**
   ☐ None, ☐ Not acceptable, ☐ Acceptable, ☐ Outstanding
   ☐ Actions needed: _____
   ☐ Assigned, ☐ Not assigned, ☐ Completion date defined

4. **Creative Process**
   Measures, Metrics and Measurements: ☐ Defined and ☐ Recorded
   Progress: ☐ Poor, ☐ Good, ☐ Excellent
   ☐ Actions needed: _____
   ☐ Assigned, ☐ Not assigned, ☐ Completion date defined

5. **Innovative Process**
   Measures, Metrics and Measurements: ☐ Defined and ☐ Recorded
   Progress: ☐ Poor, ☐ Good, ☐ Excellent
   ☐ Actions needed: _____
   ☐ Assigned, ☐ Not assigned, ☐ Completion date defined

6. **Documentation**
   ☐ Records: ☐ Made, ☐ Not made, ☐ Adequate, ☐ Not adequate
   ☐ Accessible to all team members: ☐ Yes, ☐ No, ☐ Any problems?
   ☐ Actions needed: _____
   ☐ Assigned, ☐ Not assigned, ☐ Completion date defined

Continued

Appendix F.3.   *Continued.*

7. Resources

Office Space: ☐ Available, ☐ Not available, ☐ Adequate, ☐ Not adequate
Equipment: ☐ Available, ☐ Not available, ☐ Adequate, ☐ Not adequate
Working Environment: ☐ Adequate, ☐ Not adequate
☐ Actions needed: _____
☐ Assigned, ☐ Not assigned, ☐ Completion date defined

8. Communication

Formal Meetings: ☐ Regular, ☐ Not regular, When Held: _____
Formal Meetings: ☐ Acceptable, ☐ Not acceptable, When Held: _____
Informal Meetings: ☐ Acceptable, ☐ Not Acceptable
☐ Actions Needed: _____
☐ Assigned, ☐ Not assigned, ☐ Completion date defined

9. Project Risk

Beginning: ☐ Low, ☐ Medium, ☐ High
Middle: ☐ Low, ☐ Middle, ☐ High
Near End: ☐ Low, ☐ Middle, ☐ High
☐ Actions Needed: _____
☐ Assigned, ☐ Not assigned, ☐ Completion date defined

10. Problem/Situation Statement

☐ Communicated before every creative/innovative session.
Revision needed: ☐ Yes, ☐ No

11. Presentation of Solution

☐ Dry run with all team members:
☐ Use critique Sheets
☐ Actions needed: _____
☐ Assigned, ☐ Not assigned, ☐ Completion date defined
☐ Schedule the presentation to sponsors: ☐ Date, ☐ Facilities,
☐ Projection equipment.

12. Celebration

☐ At achievement of successful milestones: ☐ Yes, ☐ No
☐ Final close of the project
☐ Successful implementation

13. Implementation

☐ If needed, transfer of project knowledge

Appendix F.4.   Patent journal format.

Date: **Location:**

Name of Journal Author:

Idea Description:

Comments:

_____   _____

Author Signature   **Date**

Understood and Witnessed by:

_____   _____

Signature   **Date**

Note: Use ink. No erasers permitted. Material to be omitted should be erased out with the strike through of a single line and initialed by the author.

Appendix G.1. Team viewpoints worksheet.

Date: **Location:**

Prepared by: **Customer:**
                          Supplier:

	Customer	Supplier
Reinforcement:		
Type preferred		
When		
Where		
Why		
By Whom		
Comments		
Recognition:		
Type preferred		
When		
Where		
Why		
By Whom		
Comments		
Rewards:		
Type preferred		
When		
Where		
Why		
By Whom		
Comments		

Appendix G.2. Co-leader reward system worksheet.

Date: **Location:**

Prepared by: **Customer:**
                   Supplier:

Reinforcement
- Type:
- When:
- Where:
- Why:
- By Whom:
- Comments:

Recognition
- Type:
- When:
- Where:
- Why:
- By Whom:
- Comments:

Rewards
- Type:
- When:
- Where:
- Why:
- By Whom:
- Comments:

Appendix G.3.   Reward system design worksheet.

Date: **Location:**

Project:

Prepared by: **Customer:**
                     Supplier:

---

1. **Purpose of Reward System:**

2. **State expected Reward System outcomes:**

3. **State how the Reward System relates to:**
   a. **Strategic results:**

   b. **Tactical results:**

   c. **Creative and Innovative tasks** (value added):

   d. **Team members critical behaviors:**

4. **State form of recognition** (Show a matrix of choices):

5. **State what will be recognized, when, by whom:**

6. **State measure, metrics and measurements to verify reward is earned by team members.**

7. **State the form of the reward** (for example, cash pay-out, gainsharing, stock options):

8. **Process to obtain input from team members regarding the reward system:**

BIBLIOGRAPHY

Altshuller, G. 1998. *40 Principles: TRIZ Keys to Technical Innovation.* Worcester, MA: Technical Innovation Center.

Amabile, T. M. 1992. *The Creative Spirit.* New York: Penguin Group. (Note: Authors Goleman, et al. Amabile cited in book.).

Amabile, T. M. 1996. *Creativity in Context.* Boulder, CO: Westview Press.

Armitage, A. 1997. "The Three Rs of Organizational Performance: Reinforcement, Recognition and Rewards." *ACA Journal.* Summer.

Baker, K. R. 1998. *Teaming on Innovation: A Brave New World for General Motors.* Warren, MI: General Motors Global R&D Operations.

Baldrige, M. 1996. *Trident Winner's Summary.* Washington, DC: NIST.

Buzan, T. 1983. *Use Both Sides of Your Brain.* New York: E. P. Dutton.

Consulting Psychologists Press Inc. 1999. Myers-Briggs Type Indicator® Inventory (MBTI)®. 3803 E. Bayshore Road, Palo Alto, CA 94303. *http://www.mbti.com.*

Daniels, J. L., and N. C. Daniels. 1993. *Global Vision.* New York: McGraw-Hill.

de Bono, E. 1992. *Serious Creativity.* New York: HarperCollins Publishing.

Deutsch. C. H. 1999. "The Deal Is Done. The Work Begins." *New York Times.* 11 April: Section 3.

Edwards, B. 1987. *Drawing on the Right Side of the Brain.* New York: Simon & Schuster.

Freudenbeger, H., and G. Pichelson. 1989. *Burn-Out: The High Cost of High Achievement.* New York: Bantam Books.

Friedman, T. L. 1999. "A Manifesto for the Fast World." *New York Times.* 28 March: 42–43.

Higgins, J. M. 1995. *Innovate or Evaporate.* Winter Park, FL: The New Management Publishing Company.

Higgins, J. M. 1994. *101 Creative Problem Solving Techniques.* Winter Park, FL: The New Management Publishing Company.

Iacocca, L. 1984. *An Autobiography: Lee Iacocca.* New York: Bantam Books.

Imai, M. 1986. *KAIZEN.* New York: McGraw-Hill.

Intel 1998. Web site. *www.intel.com.*

International Programs Center. 1999. U.S. Bureau of the Census, *http://census.gov/cgi-bin/ipc/popclockw.*

Jung, C. G. 1971. *Psychological Types.* Princeton, NJ: Princeton U.P., Bollingen Series.

Juran, J. M. 1988. *Juran on Planning for Quality.* New York: The Free Press.

Katenbach, J. R., and D. K. Smith. 1994. *The Wisdom of Teams.* New York: Harper Business.

Keen, P. 1997. *Every Manager's Guide to Business Processes.* Boston: Harvard Business School Press.

Kirton, M. J. 1994. *Adaptors and Innovators: Styles of Creativity and Problem Solving.* London: International Thomson Business Press.

Kirton, M. J. 1976. "Adaptors and Innovators: A Description and Measure." *Journal of Applied Psychology.* 61, 622–629.

Kirton, M. J. 1999. *Kirton Adaption-Innovation (KAI) Inventory.* Occupational Research Centre, 'Highlands', Gravel Path, Berkhamsted, Herts, HP42PQ, UK. Email: m.j.kirton@herts.ac.uk
http://ourworld.compuserve.com/homepages/orc_kai.

Kohn, A. 1993. *Punished by Rewards: The Trouble with Gold Stars, Incentive Plans, A's, Praise and Other Bribes.* Boston: Houghton Mifflin.

Kowalick, J. 1999. Private communication regarding TRIZ.

Levin, K. 1951. *Field, Theory and Social Science: Selected Theoretical Papers.* New York: Harper & Row.

Lewis, J. D. 1995. *The Connected Corporation: How Leading Companies Win Through Customer-Supplier Alliances.* New York: The Free Press.

Longworth, R. C. 1998. *Global Squeeze.* Chicago: Contemporary Books.

Marquardt, M. J., and A. Reynolds. 1994. *The Global Learning Organization.* Burr Ridge, IL: Irwin.

Merdith, R. 1997. "The Brave New World of General Motors," *New York Times.* 26 October: S3,12.

Minahan, T. 1997. "Allied Signal Soars by Building up Suppliers." *Purchasing.* 18 September: 41.

Minahan, T. 1998. "Chrysler Elects Procurement Team Leader As Its New President." *Purchasing.* 15 January: 25–29.

Murray, J. E. 1997. "Buying Abroad Invokes International Law Challenge." *Purchasing.* 6 November: 30–31.

NASA 1970. *http://nasdc.gsfc.nasa.gov/planetary/lunar/apollo13info.htm* and *http://www.hq.nasa.gov/office/pao/history/alsj/. Apollo Lunar Surface Journal.*

NASA 1994. *http://www.hq.nasa.gov/office/hqlibrary/ppm/ppm.29.htm.*

NASA 1999. http://hq.nasa.gov/.

Norausky, P. H. 1989. Private Communication.

Norausky, P. H. 1995. Development of the Innovation Focus Quotient, GLOMAXX, LLC.

Norausky, P. H. 1995. Development of the Organization's Innovation Focus, GLOMAXX, LLC.

Norausky, P. H. 1995. Development of the Self-Assessment for Innovation Focus, GLOMAXX, LLC.

Norausky, P. H. 1995. Private study.

Norausky, P. H. 1997. GLOMAXX, LLC. Private study.

Norausky, P. H. 1998. GLOMAXX, LLC. Private study.

Norausky, P. H. 1999A. Private communication with Michael Kirton.

Norausky, P. H. 1999B. Glass Innovation Center. The Corning Museum of Glass, Corning, NY.

Norausky, P. H. 1999C. The *3M*™ *Trizact*™ *Story.* Private communication with Stan Collins and Blane Huppert at 3M™.

Norausky, P. H. 1999D. Private communication with Frank Ceminara at Hershey Foods.

Norausky, P. H. 1999E. Private communication with GLOMAXX, LLC, regarding involvement with customer and supplier innovation teams.

Osborn, A. 1979. *Applied Imagination* (3rd rev. ed.). New York: Charles Scribner & Sons.

Patton, F. 1997. *The Quality of the Customer-Supplier Process: A Human Experience.* Atlanta, GA: Customer and Supplier Division Conference.

Penney, J. C. 1998. Web site: *www.penney.com.*

Peters, T. 1997. *The Circle of Innovation.* New York: Vintage Books.

Sage, L. 1998. Profile of Tomorrow's Automotive Supplier. Web site: *www.ey.com.*

Sheridan, J. H. 1997. "Bond of Trust." *Industry Week.* 17 March: 40–43.

Schein, E. H. 1985. *Organizational Culture and Leadership.* San Francisco: Jossey-Bass Publishers.

Schuster, J. 1984. *Management Compensation in High Technology Companies.* Lexington, MA: Lexington Books.

Skinner, B. F. 1969. *Contingencies of Reinforcement.* New York: Appleton-Century-Crofts.

Securities Data/Thomson Financial. 1999. Announced Worldwide M & A Transactions. Archieve: *www.securitiesdata.com.*

Special Advertising. 1997. Best Practices for Global Competitiveness. *Fortune.* 24 November: S2

Taylor III, A. 1999. "Kellogg Cranks Up Its Idea Machine." *Fortune.* 5 July.

Townsend, P. L., and J. E. Gebhardt. 1992. *Quality in Action.* New York: John Wiley & Sons.

Van Mieghem, T. 1995. *Implementing Supplier Partnerships.* Englewood Cliffs, NJ: Prentice Hall.

Wendal, P. 1995. "The Power of the Customer-Supplier Alliance." *The Quality Observer.* 5 December.

INDEX